Ideas That Really Work!

Activities for English and Language Arts

Cheryl Miller Thurston

Cottonwood Press, Inc.

Fort Collins, Colorado

Cottonwood Press, Inc.
109-B Cameron Drive
Fort Collins, Colorado 80525

www.cottonwoodpress.com
1-800-864-4297

ISBN 978-1-877673-84-9
Printed in the United States of America

Cover design by Rochelle Dorsey

Illustrations by Patricia Howard and Ann Blackstone

Special thanks to Laura Stanovich, a student in Brian Wedemeyer's eighth-grade honors writing class at Thunderbolt Middle School in Lake Havasu City, Arizona, for discovering an important error in the "Following Instructions" activity in an earlier edition of this book.

Table of Contents

Activities for Speech

Lessons in Grammar and Punctuation

Activities for Different Seasons

Games

Answer Keys and Sample Answers

Ideas, Ideas, Ideas

Homemade Bread & English Compositions

(or An Alternative to Correcting Papers)

C. M. Thurston

Let's suppose for a minute that you are a married woman. For health and/or economic reasons, you and your husband decide to bake all of your family's bread from now on.

You buy a bread book and try a couple of loaves. They look a little lopsided and are burned on one side, but they taste pretty good. You are pleased.

Your husband, however, becomes fascinated with the art of bread baking. He starts taking classes, reading books, trying new recipes. After a while he knows a lot about baking bread, and his loaves are a lot better than yours.

That's okay with you. However, it's not okay with him. Whenever your loaves come out of the oven, he examines them carefully. He takes notes, giving you all kinds of helpful suggestions:

* Use only stone-ground flour.
* Add a bit more water next time.
* Be more careful about the temperature of the water before you add the yeast.
* Don't forget to check the expiration date on the yeast package.
* Knead longer.
* Place the pans further apart in the oven.
* Don't forget to brush the tops with melted butter.
* Don't let the loaves cool for longer than ten minutes in the pans.

As he goes over his notes, you don't pay much attention. Perhaps a suggestion or two registers in your brain. For example, you may remember to check the expiration date on the yeast package next time. Then again, you may not. You don't really care much. Your husband is the one who cares. He puts all the effort into improving your bread—analyzing, studying, criticizing, suggesting. You let him. You also pretty much ignore him.

The quality of your bread stays essentially the same.

So what does all this have to do with English compositions? In grading compositions, many of us play the role of the bread-baking husband. We spend hours correcting every little thing on every single paper. We do all the work—analyzing, studying and suggesting. The students let us. All they do is look at their grades and, if we are lucky, perhaps give our comments and notes a passing glance as they toss them into the wastebasket.

The quality of their work stays essentially the same.

Let's face it. It is a waste of time to spend hours correcting students' compositions, especially if you want them to become better writers. When you correct their papers for them, you make them passive observers. No one becomes a better writer by glancing at someone else's corrections.

What is the alternative? A practical, easy approach is to get the students to do the correcting themselves, with your guidance.

Let's assume that you are already teaching writing as a process and that your students spend a lot of time with prewriting activities, writing and revision. You feel comfortable about all that goes into the content of your students' papers. However, you also want the students to learn to write papers that are technically correct, without errors in spelling, punctuation, sentence structure, etc. The following method is one easy way to get them actively involved in improving their own work:

- As you grade a student's paper, simply place an "x" in the margin on the line where an error occurs. An "x" in the margin means that something is wrong. (Some teachers prefer to give students more guidance at first, using "sp" for spelling errors, "frag" for sentence fragments, "?" for awkward or confusing sentences, etc. As students become more skilled at correcting their papers, the teachers switch to the more general "x.")

- When there are many errors, don't try to mark every single one of them. Instead, try to gear your marks to a student's skill level. For one student, you might use "x's" for only the worst spelling errors and for sentences that don't begin with capital letters. For another student, you might mark "x's" for more subtle things, like incorrectly punctuated dialogue. Sometimes you might decide to mark only one particular kind of error on a given paper, perhaps only run-on sentences for one student or errors in subject/verb agreement for another.

    If you start to feel guilty about not marking everything, remember your "helpful" husband in the imaginary scenario above. Wouldn't he have been more effective if he had given only one or two suggestions at a time rather than attacking everything at once? Marking too many errors may defeat your goal, overwhelming students and causing them to give up in frustration.

    And don't fall for the old argument that you must mark everything "for the parents. They will be upset if I don't. Or they will think I am lazy or that I'm not a good teacher." Your goal is not to help the parents; it is to help the students. If a parent questions your grading technique, explain what you are doing—and why. The method is perfectly defensible and gets results.

- After papers are returned, have students go over them to make corrections. Teach them to circle the place where an error occurs, writing the correction right above the circle. If a sentence needs to be rewritten, the student should circle the entire sentence and rewrite it in the margin or on the back of the page. (See sample, page 12.)

If you have students double space when they write their papers, it is even easier for them to make corrections later in the extra space.

- Allow the students time to help each other with the correction process and to receive help from you. It's also a good idea to collect examples of problems common on many papers, using the overhead or blackboard to show ways to correct the problem. (When students know they will be correcting their papers later, they will pay more attention than they might otherwise.)

- Have students turn in their corrected papers for a second, separate grade—a grade on just the corrections. Any paper with all the corrections done correctly receives the total points possible for corrections, or an "A," no matter what grade the original paper received.

As a general rule, do not have students rewrite their papers in order to do the corrections. First of all, the rewriting time is usually better spent doing something else. Second, having them rewrite the paper makes your job very difficult. You must reread the paper entirely, checking it again, or you must cross-check the original with the rewritten version to see that the corrections have been made—a time-consuming process. With the circling method, all you need to do is quickly scan a paper, looking for your "x's" in the margin and finding the circles that indicate corrections. You can learn to check the corrections for an entire class in only fifteen or twenty minutes.

If you have stressed neatness, editing and careful proofreading as part of the writing process, students will know that their final compositions should be completed with care. They will view this final correction exercise as what it really is—something separate, an exercise to help them to learn and to improve for next time.

- Emphasize that students are not to guess at corrections. It is better not to correct something at all than to "correct" it incorrectly. Allowing time for students to help each other and to ask questions will encourage them to work carefully. The reward of an "easy A" for corrections also doesn't hurt.

You will need to lead students through the correction process a time or two before they understand exactly what they are to do. Soon they are likely to view making corrections as solving a kind of puzzle. You are likely to view the process as one that saves you many hours of grading and, at the same time, helps your students become more active learners.

(continued)

A sample paper, as returned to student

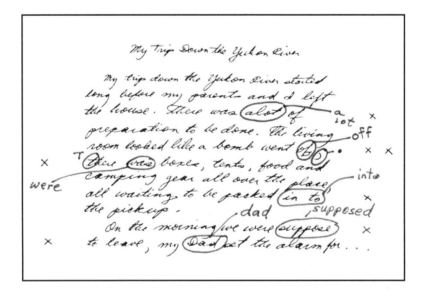

My Trip Down the Yukon River

My trip down the Yukon River started long before my parents and I left the house. There was alot of preparation to be done. The living room looked like a bomb went off, there was boxes, tents, food and camping gear all over the place, all waiting to be packed in to the pickup.

On the morning we were suppose to leave, my Dad set the alarm for...

The same paper, with student corrections

My Trip Down the Yukon River

My trip down the Yukon River started long before my parents and I left the house. There was *a lot* of preparation to be done. The living room looked like a bomb went *off*. *There* *were* boxes, tents, food and camping gear all over the place, all waiting to be packed *into* the pickup.

On the morning we were *supposed* to leave, my *dad* set the alarm for...

"I Decided to Just Teach"

C. M. Thurston

A teacher I know, who wishes to remain nameless (presumably out of modesty), started teaching last year at a school where everyone was worried about improving state test scores. Teachers were fussing, fretting, and doing everything they could think of to help their students perform well. They structured lessons around what was going to be on the test. They gave lessons in test-taking. They gave practice tests.

The teacher I know decided that she had entirely too much to worry about, as she was teaching new subjects in a new grade in a school new to her. She was overwhelmed with responsibilities. "I just plain didn't have time to worry about the tests," she said. "I decided to just teach."

At the end of the year, guess whose students made the most progress in the school, as measured by the tests?

Hers.

Okay, maybe she just lucked out. But maybe she succeeded because she did *not* focus on improving test scores. She focused on teaching and learning. Instead of boring her kids with practice tests and endless worksheets, she focused on keeping her students interested and involved. Maybe, just maybe, her approach is a sound one—to just teach.

It's something to consider.

Helping Students Help Each Other

Many teachers have tried having students evaluate each other's writing, often without much success. Students often write nothing more than "good job" on illegible papers or decorate papers indiscriminately with A's. However, there are ways to make student evaluations an important and effective part of the writing process. The key is structure.

Advantages of student evaluations. Why bother having students evaluate each other's writing? There are several reasons:

- The evaluation process gives all students an audience for their work, an audience other than the teacher. Students often respond with more effort and enthusiasm when they know their work will be read by peers.
- When students read what others have written, they often get ideas for improving their own work.
- Students can actually learn to help each other in revising and editing.
- Evaluation questions can help students focus on objectives that the teacher wants to emphasize.

Designing evaluation questions. Student evaluations work best when students are given clear goals and guidelines. Design a standard evaluation form for your students to use, or several forms to use for different purposes. Choose questions that will help your students focus on specifics, but don't include more than five or six questions, maximum, on a form.

Sometimes students are stumped by questions like, "What did you like best about the paper?" Help them out by having the class brainstorm a list of possible responses, things like "Interesting to read," "This made me laugh," "Good detail," "I like the paragraph about _____," "Exciting," "Nice handwriting," "Well-organized," etc.

Here are sample evaluation questions for an eighth grade class learning to write simple essays:

1. This paper was evaluated by:
2. Do you see spelling, capitalization or punctuation errors? If so, in what lines?
3. Does the paper have a paragraph of introduction?
4. What do you like best about the paper?
5. What do you like least about the paper?
6. What suggestions do you have for the author?

Other ideas for evaluation questions:

1. Do you see any sentence fragments or run-on sentences? If so, where?
2. What paragraph uses the most interesting verbs? List some of those verbs.
3. Does the paper "drag" or become boring at any point? If so, where?
4. Is any part of the paper confusing to you? If so, explain.
5. Are the sentences too short and choppy? If so, what lines give some examples?
6. Is there a sentence in the introduction that grabs your attention and makes you want to read on? If so, which sentence is it?

Using student evaluations in your classroom.
Prepare for student evaluations by having each student come to class with a clearly readable draft of his or her paper, whether it's a paragraph, a story or a complete composition. Emphasize that the paper should not be the final copy.

Have the students number each line of their papers, putting the numbers in the margin. Discuss the questions on the evaluation form with the students.

Give each student several evaluation forms, and then have students start trading papers. Allow time for each student to read and evaluate at least two papers.

At the end of the evaluation time, return each paper with all its evaluation forms to the author. Allow students to ask questions of their evaluators and to help one another in making corrections and changes in their work. Stress that students should consider each evaluator's comments and suggestions, but that they may, of course, choose to ignore them. The author of each paper is the final judge of what to change and what to leave the same.

Have students write their final drafts, incorporating all changes and corrections that they feel are relevant.

Having realistic expectations.
Don't worry too much if some students don't seem to take the evaluation process very seriously or if some of their comments are completely off the mark. The important thing is that students will be reading each other's work, seeing how others approach various topics and—as they go over the evaluation questions for others—learning some important techniques for improving their own work. They will also be learning to evaluate others' criticism of their work, judging the value of comments for themselves, and learning the important lesson that they can disagree with suggestions and reject them.

Vocabulary Study Doesn't Need to Be Boring

Words are fascinating. Learning new words can be immensely rewarding, giving a person greater understanding of the world, more confidence and even a sense of power.

Why then is vocabulary study so frequently a dull activity that students hate? Too often it is because we, as teachers, simply repeat the same assignment we received ourselves as students:

Look up the word in the dictionary. Copy the definition.
Use the word in a sentence. Study. Take a test.

Sometimes the method works for a few students, especially the ones who actually understand the dictionary definitions they memorize. For most students, however, the assignment results in only minimal vocabulary development.

There are ways to make vocabulary study a lively, highly effective activity for students. If any of the ideas below are new to you, consider giving them a try.

- Don't have the students copy dictionary definitions. Instead, use a given vocabulary word orally in several sentences, and have the class guess its meaning. Decide together on an accurate definition that the students really understand, using informal language, even slang, if necessary. Consult the dictionary for assistance, but use it only as a resource. As the students "discover" the meaning of a word, they will become actively involved in learning it.

- Don't overdo it. Choose only a few words at a time for a class to study, probably five or ten and certainly no more than twenty. Then stick with those words until you are confident that your students know them well. You will probably wind up assigning far fewer words than the teacher down the hall and giving tests less frequently, but that's all right. Your students will really *learn* the words they study, rather than just memorizing definitions for a test.

- Choose realistic words. Don't fall into the trap of choosing obscure words mentioned in the footnotes to a story you are reading in class. The story may mention "chiasmatypy," but how many of us need to know that word more than once or twice in a lifetime, if ever? Instead, choose words that you see and hear frequently. Jot down words students seemed puzzled by in class reading or discussion. Allow students themselves to suggest words they are unsure about. Look ahead and choose useful words from materials your students will be reading later in the year. Choose your words from a variety of sources, always keeping one question uppermost in your mind: *Is this a word students really need to know?*

- Recognize that learning new words has nothing to do with spelling. All of us need to recognize and understand many words that we will never actually write or need to spell ourselves. We need to achieve a level of comfort with a word before we ever even consider using it ourselves. Therefore, it is best not to test for spelling in a vocabulary test. Make your tests a measure of your real objective, vocabulary improvement.

  That does not mean that you should ignore incorrect spelling. Insist that students spell the words correctly on their papers and on their tests, but allow them access to the correct spellings. (Sometimes getting them even to copy correctly is an achievement!)

- Help your students become actively involved in using the words they study. Have them write stories using all the words on a list. (Understand that the stories may have to be fairly outrageous to include all the words.) Give students an assignment to use at least three vocabulary words outside of class. Then let individuals report what they said, and to whom.

  Play little games at the end of class: Who can use the first and last words on the list in a meaningful sentence? Who can ask a question using one of the words? Who can answer it, using another? Who can use one of the words in a sentence about a dog? A football game? A television show? (Don't allow the generic "He was _____." Instead, insist that the sentence itself give a clue about the meaning of the word.)

  Don't worry when a student clearly knows the meaning of a word but uses it in a slightly bizarre fashion. Refinements in usage will come later. The first step is to learn the meaning of the word.

- Try using a vocabulary point system. Keep track of vocabulary points a class earns and assign some reward to those points. A certain number of points earned in a quarter might earn a game day or a class treat, for example. A point system can encourage involvement by all class members.

  A few ideas you might try: Offer ten points if someone can define all the words on a new list. See how far you can go around the room, with students giving correct definitions; then give points for the number of students who answered correctly. Every now and then, allow five minutes for students to report on "sightings" or "hearings" of vocabulary words. Give points, for example, if they tell how a word was used by Lesley Stahl on *60 Minutes*, or by the author of their science textbook, or by Randy in the first row's mother.

- Have fun with your tests. For example, you might write a story, leaving blanks for students to fill in with the vocabulary words and using students as characters in the story. With a computer, it is easy to change the names in the story to fit each class. Students learn to look forward to tests that are both challenging and fun to read.

Cars in Class

Kids share America's love of the automobile. Young teenagers long for the day they are old enough to drive. They dream about having cars of their own. They envy older teenagers who work at part-time jobs, just to make car payments. They fantasize about having a car they think will make them irresistible to the opposite sex—and about just what they might do in the back seat of such a car!

Teachers can capitalize on their students' interest in cars, using the subject to draw students into a number of activities. Even apathetic students will often respond to lessons centered around the automobile.

One effective way to bring cars into the language arts classroom is through advertisements. Have your students collect a variety of magazine advertisements for cars, trucks and vans. After everyone has had an opportunity to study several ads, use them for a variety of language-related activities. Below are just a few ideas.

Grammar.

Have students look for adjectives and/or verbs in the advertisements the class has collected. List the most effective or interesting verbs and adjectives in two different columns on the board, creating a word bank that students can use later when they write their own ads.

Also have students look for sentence fragments in the ads. They will probably find a lot of them. Like it or not, there is a trend in advertising to break sentences into pieces, presumably for emphasis. Students may protest that they don't need to know how to write complete sentences, if even professional writers write sentence fragments. In that case, here is your answer for them: *Professional writers are consciously breaking the rules, for an intended purpose. They know what they are doing. Breaking the rules out of ignorance rarely achieves the same purpose.*

You might compare writing to dancing. Have the students imagine the kind of dancing they see on music videos or at rock concerts. A very basic "rule" of dancing is that it is not a good idea to fall down in the middle of a dance. If an inexperienced or ill-prepared dancer falls down in the middle of a performance, the performance is probably judged a failure by anyone seeing it. However, if a skilled dancer chooses to fall in a performance, as a planned part of a routine, the result can be quite effective. It is clear to the audience, however, that the fall is part of the choreography, not a sloppy error.

Discussion/critical thinking.

Finding sentence fragments in advertising can lead easily into a discussion of how advertisers break many other rules. Discuss the kinds of errors frequently seen in ads: spelling mistakes, double negatives, using "like" instead of "as," etc. Ask students to imagine why the rules are intentionally broken. (Some possible answers: to catch the reader's attention, to reflect the way people actually talk, to be "cute.") Discuss whether or not all the intentional errors have an effect on language in this country, or on children learning to read and write.

Another discussion idea is to talk about the different images advertisers help create for cars. Which vehicles, for example, are associated with soccer moms? Which ones have a "young" image, or a "sexy" image, or a "daring" image, or a "reliable" image, or a "family" image? How do advertisers help create those images? Are the images always based on reality?

If you have older students, you might discuss sex and sexism in advertisements. What does a woman in a bikini have to do with the qualities of a four-wheel drive pick-up truck? What are other ways that advertisers use sex to influence consumers? You might find some old ads from the 1950s or 1960s, ads that assume a woman can't possibly be interested in anything more than an automobile's color. Have students compare those ads with the ads today that address female consumers.

You might also have students discuss values. Ask them to imagine they are foreigners looking at American automobile ads. Do the ads tell anything about American values? If so, what? How do students feel about those values?

After class discussion on various topics related to automobile advertising, ask students to explore their ideas further in writing.

Creative writing.
Students can let their imaginations run wild when they try this assignment: Design a car with a specific kind of person in mind. One student might want to design the perfect automobile for a sixteen-year-old boy, both from the boy's perspective and from the perspective of his parents. Another might want to design a car for the owner of a preschool, for a certain television star, for a skier, or for a teacher.

Have students draw the cars they design and then create magazine ads for the cars. Besides exercising their creativity, they will need to think about and address some important areas:

- Who is their intended audience?
- How can their writing best appeal to that audience?
- How can they get their intended readers' attention?
- What are the main points they want to emphasize in an ad?
- How can they be clear and concise, saying a lot in just a small amount of space?
- What headlines would best help them convey the message they want to convey?

When students finish, post the finished ads around the room. Have students discuss which ads are most effective in "selling" their cars.

Just for fun.
For a break in routine, have students try the game "Cars" (page 20).

Cars

Directions

For each category listed along the side of the page, think of an appropriate word that begins with the letter at the top of the page. The first item is done for you.

	C	**A**	**R**	**S**
Makes of cars	Chevrolet			
Adjectives that describe cars				
Colors of cars				
Verbs that tell what a car does				
Parts of a car				
Adverbs that tell how someone might drive a car				
Cities in America where you might drive a car				

Imagine That . . .

C. M. Thurston

When I was growing up, I dreamed of learning to ice-skate. I imagined myself leaping, spinning, skimming over a frozen lake, graceful and, of course, breathtakingly beautiful as well. Unfortunately, I happened to grow up on the hot, dry plains of southern Colorado. Frozen lakes weren't in the picture. Actually, lakes weren't even in the picture. My childhood dream of gracefulness went unfulfilled, as did the breathtakingly beautiful part of the fantasy.

But many years later, as an adult, I received a pair of ice skates for Christmas. They weren't ordinary ice skates, the kind a non-skater like me would expect to receive. They were expensive ice skates, the kind of ice skates that expected to find feet that knew what they were doing. They were ice skates that made me nervous. I wasn't the athletic type. What if I turned out to have no talent at all for skating? I decided, out of guilt, that I had to learn to skate. I couldn't let those expensive skates go to waste.

> "True success is overcoming the fear of being unsuccessful."
> – Paul Sweeney

The pressure was on. I checked some books out of the library and read about ice-skating. I imagined myself doing what the people in the pictures were doing. I watched ice skaters on television. I imagined myself performing with grace and agility. I thought about my first lesson. I imagined myself putting on the skates, getting up and gliding away.

Finally, I visited some friends with a small, frozen pond near their home. Nervously, I trooped with my friends and their small children—all skaters—down to the ice. I put on my skates. I got up. I skated.

I couldn't believe it. No one watching could believe it. I didn't fall down once. Again and again, I skated around the pond, thrilled by my success. No, I wasn't the vision of loveliness and grace I had imagined, but I was skating. I was actually skating.

> "I am what I think, having become what I thought."
> – Unknown

This incident made me a believer in the power of imagination. Perhaps, to succeed at something, we must first be able to imagine it. It worked with ice-skating. And it works with other more important areas of life.

Take a look at the quotations on this page. Think about them. Think about them in relation to your students. Think about the students who seem to be wearing an ever-deeper path toward failure. They can't seem to veer off the path in another direction. The present path feels familiar to them; they know what to expect; they can deal with it. They can't do things differently because they can't even *imagine* doing things differently.

(continued)

Think about the students who seem aimless, coasting through life without goals, direction, hopes or dreams. Think about the students who won't even try in school. They can't conceive of success at anything, so why attempt it? And think about the students who do try but who have trouble with so much they attempt. Something seems to hold them back.

The exercise that follows is an interesting experiment to try with your students. Besides providing the basis for thought-provoking classroom discussion and writing, it may actually give students a tool to use in setting and achieving goals.

Discussing positive goals.
First, talk with your students about goals they have had in the past. What goals have they met? What goals have they failed to meet?

Talk about the difference between positive and negative goals. A negative goal is one that is destructive. It hurts someone. A positive goal is constructive. It takes a person or group forward in some meaningful way. It builds rather than tears down.

> "What you can *conceive* and *believe*, you can *achieve*."
> – Unknown

Ask your students to think about positive goals they may already have for themselves. If they have no goals, ask them to think about the subject and to come up with three goals that would be meaningful to them. Encourage students to choose goals that really are important to them, rather than just going through the motions to fulfill an assignment.

The goals they choose might be in any areas they find important. A few examples: habits, school, sports, church, friends, family, work. Although they need not share all their goals, ask students to have at least one in mind that they don't mind sharing with other members of the class.

Talking about success.
After students have their goals in mind, ask for volunteers to share some of their goals. Have class members share suggestions for reaching those goals.

Next, share the quotations from the previous page of this article. Ask students to discuss their thoughts about the quotations.

Finally, ask students to sit quietly and imagine that they have completed one of their goals, the goal they don't mind sharing with the class. Ask them to project themselves into the future and to pretend they have been successful. Ask them these questions: How does it feel to have achieved your goal? What has been the reaction of others? Do you feel you have

> "It may be those who do most, dream most."
> – S. Leacock

changed in any way? How? Would you do this over again? How would you do things differently next time? How are you going to celebrate?

Have the students do some role-playing, either as a class or in small groups. Have the students talk to their groups about how it feels to have met their goals. Encourage them to ham it up if they like. This is a time to feel good and to do a bit of bragging.

Writing about success.
Have students continue their role-playing on paper, writing about their imagined success at meeting a goal, their feelings, their reactions, the reactions of others. Remind them that they are to write as if they have already accomplished the goal, as if it were already a "done deal."

Finally, ask students to keep their papers and to read them again from time to time. Encourage them to share their successes with the class as they meet goals and to tell whether or not they think the imagining exercise had any effect on helping them reach their goals.

Helping Students Learn to Appreciate Differences

Young people are sometimes not the most tolerant of human beings. Just let someone seem the slightest bit different or "weird," and students attack, teasing or taunting unmercifully. To teenagers in particular, it is important to fit in, to be accepted, to conform—except when it comes to conforming to teacher or parent expectations.

A language arts unit built around the theme "appreciating differences" can be a useful and interesting unit for students. It can help them become more sensitive toward those who seem different. It can help them see the similarities between all human beings and even take pride in their own differences.

Most literature anthologies include at least one story about a person who is different, or who takes an unpopular stand. You can select stories from the materials you have available in your classroom and read aloud from other works. In addition to reading and discussing literature about people who are different, you might choose ideas from the following activities:

- Have speakers talk to the class about how they were different as teenagers. For example, a successful business person might talk about how he or she couldn't pass algebra in high school and felt stupid. A model or television personality might talk about how he or she felt ugly as a teenager and was taunted because of braces, height, weight, etc. A teacher from a minority group might talk about difficulties he or she faced attending a mostly-white college. A community leader might talk about struggling with a learning disability or other handicap while growing up.

  Speakers who are willing to talk candidly about earlier problems can help students in two ways: (1) they can encourage students to become more sensitive to the feelings of others, and (2) their words can give encouragement to those feeling different themselves.

- Have students question each other, looking for something that makes each person absolutely unique, different from everyone else in class. Students might work in pairs, using questions the class has previously brainstormed. Students might find that a partner is the only one in the class who has lived in Alaska, plays the dulcimer, once won a beautiful baby contest, or has five brothers. Volunteers might make a bulletin board, posting something unique about each person in the class. (Note: Explain to students ahead of time that they may choose not to answer some questions by simply saying, "pass." Explain also that each student must also okay anything to be shared with the class.)

- Have the class read aloud and discuss the article "Eccentrics" (page 25). The composition assignment "Everyone is Different" (page 27) is a natural follow-up activity.

Eccentrics

According to an old saying, only the rich are called "eccentric;" the poor are simply called "crazy." Is there any truth to the saying? That is a matter of opinion.

It is true that every community has individuals who fit the description of an eccentric—someone who is decidedly different, who is considered odd or out of the ordinary, who does the unexpected.

There have been many eccentrics throughout history, some famous and some not so famous. One of the more well-known was Nikola Tesla, a scientist, inventor and electrical engineer who is sometimes known as the patron saint of modern electricity. The number of any hotel room he stayed in had to be divisible by the number three. He didn't like to touch anything round, and jewelry revolted him, especially pearl earrings.

Less well-known was William Henry Schmidt, who spent 32 years tunneling through a mountain. Early in the twentieth century, Schmidt found a vein of gold in California's Copper Mountain. He decided to tunnel through the mountain so that he could have easy access to a road to the smelter. In 1906 he started cutting through a half-mile of solid granite, using only hand tools and sometimes dynamite. He worked seven days a week, sleeping only when fatigue overtook him. It wasn't until 1938, 32 years after he had started, that he made it through to the other side.

Another eccentric was Hetty Green, a nineteenth-century millionaire banker who lived in poverty with her two children. She didn't want to waste money on soap, so she washed only the lower part of her long skirts. She stuffed her son's clothes with newspapers to keep out the wind. Once she was furious to be charged ten cents for a bottle of medicine and thereafter brought her own bottle to save five cents. Worst of all, she tried to save money on medical

(continued)

treatment when her son had a sledding accident and dislocated his kneecap. Because of the resulting infection, the boy had to have his leg amputated.

The son, Ned Green, became an eccentric in his own right. After his mother's death, he managed to spend over three million dollars a year until he died. At that time, he was still worth over 50 million dollars.

Florence Foster Jenkins (1868-1944) was an American soprano who became famous for having absolutely no singing ability. She is said to have had little rhythm and couldn't stay on pitch. Still, she became quite popular, mostly because people were amused by her. She was quite convinced that she was a rare talent and dismissed laughter during her performances as coming from other singers with "professional jealousy."

Another eccentric was Ferdinand Waldo Demara, Jr., a high school dropout who specialized in impersonating different professions. He was an expert at forging documents, giving false references and teaching himself advanced concepts. He fooled experts in many fields and at various times worked successfully as a soldier, a biologist involved in cancer research, a professor teaching college psychology courses, a Trappist monk, and even a doctor, performing successful surgery.

For further discussion

- Tell the class about an eccentric person, someone who does not go to your school. It might be an eccentric person you have known, your parents have known, or that you have read about. Do not use the person's name. Here are some questions you might answer in telling about the person: What does he or she do that is out of the ordinary? How do others react to the person? Does the person seem happy? Does the person seem to have a sense of humor or a kind of genius about something? Does he or she have an obsession, an unusual interest of some kind?

  (Note: Be considerate of people's feelings. Don't tell about anything that would embarrass someone.)

- People often focus on the negative when it comes to talking about or dealing with eccentric people. After the class has shared stories about eccentric people, try looking at the positive side of things. What is positive about the eccentric lives of the people you heard about? How do they positively affect the people around them, or the world around them? What can others learn from them?

Everyone Is Different

Every person on earth is a unique individual. Every person has characteristics that make him or her different from everyone else. Some of these characteristics are certain to be considered abnormal, unusual, different or even "weird," at least by some people.

The fact is that every person really is an individual. There is something about every person that others would find unusual. Differences are what make people interesting.

- With your class, brainstorm a list of famous people, past and present. Choose a person you are interested in, and then go to the library and start reading about him or her. Try to find something unusual about the person's life. Did the person have difficulties to overcome? A handicap? An unusual upbringing? Strange habits? Unusual beliefs?

  Write a paragraph describing the most unusual fact you discovered in your reading. Be sure to note the sources of your information at the end of the paragraph.

- Now write about yourself and how you are unique. What makes you different from most people your age? You might consider any of these areas that apply: ideas, personality traits, fears, hopes, dreams, problems, experiences, interests, or background. Consider any difference that sets you apart, including those that others may not know about.

  How do you deal with the ways you are different? Do you try to hide your differences? Are you proud of them? Ashamed of them? Afraid of them? Would you change them if you could? Why or why not?

Following Instructions

To help your students understand the importance of following instructions, set aside a class period or two to address the subject. An effective introduction to the topic is "Following Instructions: A Test" (page 30), which includes the instruction to "Read all of the items below, #1-#25, before you begin." If the students do—which is unlikely—they will see that item #25 instructs them to complete only items #1, #2 and #3.

Before giving the test, be sure to mention that some students may already have taken a similar test at some time. (There are a number of different versions around.) Stress that those students are not to say anything, but to go ahead and complete the test again, sitting quietly when finished.

Most students will rush through the test, completing the items that tell them to shout, hum, draw, add, subtract, etc. After the time is up, see if anyone really did follow the instructions, completing only items #1, #2 and #3.

Discussion. The test will provide a natural lead-in to a discussion about following instructions. Ask students if they can think of some times when it is important to follow instructions. List their responses on the board or overhead. (Possible responses: on the job, when taking tests, putting together models, learning a computer program, following recipes.)

Then ask them to think of some of the consequences of not following instructions. (Possible responses: getting in trouble, losing a job, getting a bad grade, embarrassing oneself, not getting a promotion, causing injury or loss of life.)

Choosing NOT to follow instructions. At some point, students are likely to say, "But what if I don't want to follow instructions?" You can explain that it is important to understand the difference between choosing not to follow instructions and not following them because of error, inattention, or misunderstanding.

Sometimes there may be good reasons for not following instructions. For example, a person might want to experiment with a new method of completing a task. Or a person might believe it better to follow his or her conscience. Ask the students to think of times it would be wrong to follow instructions. (Possible responses: being instructed by your boss to do something illegal, having superiors instruct you to do something immoral, following instructions that you believe will result in harm or injury to another.)

Helpful hints. Following instructions accurately is a skill that is useful in so many situations. Ask students to brainstorm ideas that might help them do a better job of following instructions. If they don't come up with the following helpful hints, be sure to point them out:

- For oral instructions, listen carefully. Take notes if possible.

- Imagine yourself doing each task as the instructions are given. Create a mental picture in your mind.

- If there is any part of the instructions you don't understand, be sure to ask questions.

- For written instructions, read or at least skim over everything, to make sure there are no surprises.

- Proceed one step at a time. Sometimes worrying about later steps will just confuse you, especially when later tasks are based upon earlier ones. Something that doesn't make a lot of sense now may make more sense by the time you reach that step.

- Check off each task as it is completed.

- Review your work, making sure you have completed all instructions.

Following Instructions: A Test

Directions. This is a test on following instructions. You will have exactly ten minutes to complete the test. Be sure to read all of the items below, #1-#25, before you begin.

1. Write your name at the top, right-hand corner of this paper, in the space provided.
2. Draw a star after your name.
3. Sign your name at the bottom, center, of this page, using your normal handwriting.
4. Draw a hat on the face in the left-hand margin.
5. Write the alphabet in small letters, across the bottom of this page.
6. Divide 786 by 2. Put the answer here:
7. Softly hum the tune to "Row, Row, Row Your Boat" as you complete item #8.
8. Draw horizontal stripes in the triangle in the right-hand margin.
9. Add your zip code to the year you were born. Put the answer here:
10. If you get this far, repeat these words aloud, three times: "One-third finished!"
11. Draw a heart inside the box in the right-hand margin.
12. What is your favorite color? Write it here:
13. Turn around and smile at the person seated behind you. If no one is seated behind you, smile at your teacher.
14. Write down the name of any teacher you had last year:
15. Spell out your middle name, backwards. (If you don't have a middle name, spell out your last name, backwards.)
16. Stand up and stretch. You deserve a break.
17. Which do you like better, dogs or cats? Write your answer here:
18. Draw a tiny circle in the bottom, right-hand corner of this page.
19. What is your favorite television program? Write your answer here:
20. Write down the seventh, fourteenth and twenty-third letters of the alphabet:
21. If you get this far, shout these words: "I'm going to finish on time! I'm going to finish on time!"
22. Turn this page over and draw a large house.
23. If the house you drew doesn't have a chimney, draw one. Then draw smoke coming out of it.
24. Subtract 39 from 2567. Write the answer here:
25. Complete only items #1, #2 and #3 above. Ignore items #4-24.

Cartoon Prose

Most students love cartoons a lot more than they love English classes. That's why it's often effective to build lessons around comic strips. Besides getting students' attention, the comics can inject a bit of humor into otherwise routine classroom exercises.

Here's just one idea: Give students copies of short cartoon strips, preferably ones with a lot of action. Then have them turn the dialogue into prose. In other words, students will communicate what is happening in the cartoon strip, but without using any drawings.

Students will need to set the stage first. Where are the cartoon characters? What are they doing? Examples:

Jon stands with Garfield waiting to hear the results of the cat show competition.

Charlie Brown stands on the pitcher's mound. His face is turning red, and he is sweating.

The words in the cartoon dialogue "bubbles" will become paragraphs of dialogue, with quotation marks and words like "he says" or "she asks" to indicate who is saying what. Remind students that they should change paragraphs each time speakers change. Examples:

> *The announcer says, "And the winner of the household cat division is...Garfield!"*
> *Jon's face breaks into a wide smile. He turns to Garfield and says, "Congratulations, Garfield. Did you ever think you could win a cat show?"*
> *Garfield rolls his eyes. "Does a baby go 'goo'?"*

> *"Good grief," sighs Charlie.*
> *"Are you ready?" calls Lucy sweetly. There is a nasty grin on her face.*
> *"I'm as ready as I'll ever be," he answers.*

This exercise gives students practice constructing sentences and punctuating dialogue. It also provides an excellent way for inexperienced writers to gain some experience writing and punctuating sentences properly, without having to come up with subject matter on their own. The cartoon strips provide a framework. The students construct the sentences around that framework.

(Note: Before turning students loose, it's a good idea to demonstrate by completing one cartoon strip explanation yourself, either on the overhead projector or as a handout.)

(continued)

Cartoon Time

I'VE GOT IT! I KNOW HOW TO GET MY STUDENTS' ATTENTION! I'LL TRY BUILDING MY LESSONS AROUND COMICS! COMIC STRIPS! JOKES! CARTOONS! YES!

NOW YOU'RE THINKING. AFTER ALL, COMICS ARE A FORM OF COMMUNICATION — A POPULAR FORM. THERE IS SO MUCH YOU CAN DO WITH THEM...

LIKE WHAT? YOU'RE THE TEACHER FAIRY. GIVE ME SOME IDEAS.

YOUR WISH IS MY COMMAND....

1ST PREPARE

- FIRST FILL YOUR ROOM WITH COMIC STRIPS AND CARTOONS. PUT COLORFUL SUNDAY COMICS ON THE WALLS.
- BRING IN CARTOON BOOKS (THE FAR SIDE, CALVIN AND HOBBES, DOONESBURY, BLOOM COUNTY AND OTHER COLLECTIONS).
- PUT COPIES OF YOUR FAVORITE CARTOONS ON THE BULLETIN BOARDS.
- HAVE STUDENTS BRING IN THEIR OWN FAVORITE CARTOONS, AND POST THOSE.
- ALSO, FOR A LATER ASSIGNMENT, HAVE STUDENTS SUBMIT WRITTEN JOKES — JOKES THAT AREN'T RACIST OR SEXIST OR OFF-COLOR.

(continued)

THEN TALK ABOUT CARTOONS

NEXT, HAVE YOUR STUDENTS TAKE A SERIOUS LOOK AT CARTOONS:

- WHAT KINDS OF CARTOONS ARE THERE? (ONE-FRAME JOKES, SHORT DAILY STRIPS, SERIAL STRIPS WITH A CONTINUING STORY LINE, ETC.)

- WHAT DEVICES DO CARTOONISTS USE?

FOR DIALOGUE   FOR IDEAS   FOR SWEARING

FOR DREAMING OR THINKING   TO INDICATE MOTION   ETC.

- HOW DO CARTOON STYLES DIFFER? (REALISTIC AND DETAILED LIKE PRINCE VALIANT; DISTORTED LIKE THE SIMPSONS, ETC.)

- WHAT EXAGGERATIONS ARE OFTEN USED IN CARTOONS? (LARGE HEADS, LARGE EYES, TINY LEGS, ETC.)

- WHAT MAKES A CARTOON DIFFERENT FROM A WRITTEN STORY OR JOKE? (THE PICTURES TELL MUCH OF THE STORY; DIALOGUE IS USED EXTENSIVELY; SIMPLICITY IS IMPORTANT; COMMUNICATION MUST BE CRISP AND TO THE POINT; ETC.)

- WHAT KINDS OF CARTOONS DO YOU FIND MOST APPEALING?

- WHAT ARE YOUR FAVORITE CARTOONS? WHAT DO YOU LIKE MOST ABOUT THEM?

BUILD CLASSROOM ACTIVITIES AROUND CARTOONS

CHOOSE A SHORT CARTOON STRIP WITH A LOT OF ACTION. HAVE STUDENTS REWRITE THE STRIP INTO PROSE, USING WORDS TO COMMUNICATE THE VISUAL DETAILS AND PUNCTUATING AND PARAGRAPHING THE DIALOGUE CORRECTLY.

HAVE EACH STUDENT CHOOSE A FAVORITE CARTOON CHARACTER AND WRITE A CHARACTER SKETCH. (OPUS, CALVIN, CATHY, BATMAN, ETC.)

PHOTOCOPY A PAGE FULL OF CARTOONS, BUT WITHOUT THE DIALOGUE. DRAW IN LARGE BALLOONS AND LET STUDENTS CREATE APPROPRIATE DIALOGUE. IT'S FUN TO SEE HOW CREATIVE THEY CAN BE AND TO COMPARE THEIR CARTOONS WITH THE ORIGINALS. OFTEN, THEIR OWN VERSIONS WILL BE FUNNIER THAN THE ORIGINALS.

HAVE STUDENTS TURN WRITTEN JOKES INTO CARTOONS, ALLOWING THEM TO CHOOSE THEIR JOKES FROM THOSE COLLECTED EARLIER.

HAVE STUDENTS MAKE THEIR OWN "CLASSIC COMICS," BASED UPON A SHORT STORY OR BOOK THEY HAVE STUDIED. EXPLAIN THAT THEY WILL HAVE ONLY A CERTAIN NUMBER OF PAGES TO HELP STUDENTS WHO HAVEN'T READ THE STORY TO UNDERSTAND ITS IMPORTANT ELEMENTS—

HAVE STUDENTS WORK IN SMALL GROUPS TO CREATE AN IDEA FOR A COMIC STRIP TO APPEAL TO A SPECIFIC GROUP. (SKATE-BOARDERS, CHILDREN OF DIVORCE, TAP DANCERS, HUNTERS, DROP-OUTS, COUCH POTATOES, WHATEVER...) EACH GROUP MEMBER COULD THEN CREATE A SAMPLE OF THE STRIP TO "SELL" TO AN APPROPRIATE NEWSPAPER OR MAGAZINE.

(continued)

Have each student create a "public service" comic strip that gives a clear message. (Examples: Don't smoke. Don't use drugs. Drive safely and soberly.)

Bring in a cartoonist to talk to the class. The local newspaper might be able to help, or perhaps local artists can help you locate someone.

Show a movie on how animated films are made.

Have students do some research on cartoonists like Walt Disney, Gary Larson, Berke Breathed, Charles Schulz, etc. — or on animation, the comic book industry, the history of comics, etc. They might summarize their results in short oral talks or written reports.

Give a lesson on how to draw cartoons, even if you aren't an artist...

DRAWING DRIPS

You don't have to be an artist to draw cartoons. Anyone can draw drips, which are very simple & adaptable cartoon characters —

First, draw what looks like a drop of water. (It's all right if it's lopsided)

Add legs if you want.....

Or arms......

Make big eyes ..... The eyes are important.

You may add a mouth, if you want...

Now experiment by drawing drips with eyes and/or mouths in different positions. Try to make your drips show different emotions — sadness, excitement, anger, joy, etc....

Next try to draw different drip characters — a gorgeous drip, a handsome drip, a baby drip, a punk drip, etc.

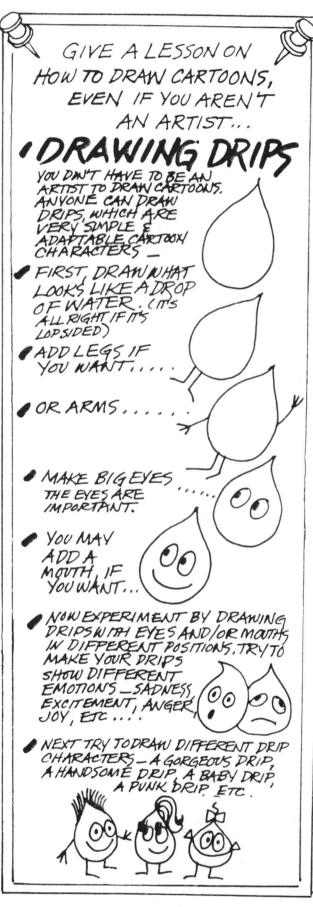

The Truth vs. the Whole Truth

Is something true just because someone says it is? Of course not. However, sometimes even a true statement can be very misleading.

Let's suppose that Jared says, "My parents won't give me any lunch money, so I've been hungry all week." That statement makes the parents sound rather heartless. Jared may be telling the truth, but he may have left out some information—that he is supposed to make his own lunch from food at home, but he's too lazy to do it. Or that he is supposed to use his allowance for lunch, but he spent it all on music downloads. This added information can change our impression of the parents.

For each statement below, see if you can imagine information the speaker might have left out, information that would change the impression each statement leaves.

1. Mom grounded me for a month, just because I didn't empty the dishwasher.
2. David gave his little sister a black eye.
3. Victoria's parents won't let her go to school.
4. Mr. Barton had to pick his daughter up at the police station at 4:00 a.m.
5. Felicia's mother lost all her money in a poker game.
6. We didn't do our homework because the substitute teacher told us not to.
7. The teacher told my daughter she couldn't write her research paper on polar bears, but she let another girl write on polar bears.
8. My dad won't let me go out with Robert anymore, just because he got a tattoo.

A statement can be true yet leave a false impression. Sometimes there is a difference between the truth and the whole truth. Have you ever deliberately told only part of the truth to someone—perhaps to your parents or to a teacher? Have you ever been misled because you heard only part of the truth? How can people guard against being misled by statements that leave out important information?

You Can Prove Anything If You Want

Many years ago, an old man was murdered in a small Colorado town. The leading suspect was a high school senior in the town. As soon as the boy was brought in for questioning, people began talking. Nearly everyone was convinced that the boy had done it. Why? There was a great deal of evidence.

First of all, those on his bowling team remembered that the boy was absent the night of the murder, and he had never been absent before. Teachers remembered that the boy had often been in trouble at school. A number of people had seen the boy in the neighborhood on the afternoon of the killing. And, finally, the boy had no alibi for the evening.

According to rumor, the boy was guilty. But was he really? No. The police eventually discovered that the murder had been committed by a man who had escaped from a mental institution. What about all the "evidence" that the boy was guilty?

As it turned out, he had stayed home from bowling because he had the flu. He had been seen in the neighborhood the afternoon of the killing because his girlfriend lived near there. Yes, he often got into trouble at school, but so did a lot of other students. That didn't mean he had murdered someone. And he couldn't prove where he was the evening of the murder because his parents had been out of town.

Unfortunately, it is often easy to "prove" things that aren't true. If you look for evidence for what you want to see, you will probably be able to find it. You may, however, have to ignore a lot of evidence to the contrary.

Try the following experiment. Find all the evidence you can to "prove" one of the false statements listed below. List your "evidence" in complete sentences.

1. Your teacher robbed a bank last week.
2. There is a secret training center for U.S. spies in your town.
3. A relative of the Loch Ness monster is sleeping in a local swimming pool at night.
4. The school cafeteria is haunted.

It is possible to "prove" statements that are actually false. How can you apply this knowledge to the real world? Think about television, newspapers, books, speeches, conversations, etc. Why is it important for people to read and listen critically?

The "M"-ey Awards

Words You Love

C. M. Thurston

When I was in fourth grade, my class studied Mexico. All I remember was learning about the volcano, Popocatépetl (po-po-cah-TEH-petl). I loved the popcorny, rhythmic sound of the word and found myself chanting it to myself, over and over again.

A few years later, I studied Frank Lloyd Wright's famous home, "Taliesin" (tal-ee-ES-in). Again, I was smitten—not with the subject but with the name itself. This time I loved the perfect, flowing, melodic sound of the name. I thought it was beautiful.

Then I became intrigued with the word "scratch." It isn't a pretty word, but it is such an oddly scrunched word—so many sounds bumping into one another to create a grating sound that perfectly fits the meaning of the word.

What words have caught your attention over the years? Do you remember learning a new word and then using it all the time? Have you ever found that you have been pronouncing a word incorrectly for years? Are there words you can't remember how to spell, or how to pronounce, no matter what you do? (I'll never learn to say the word "chignon," for example. I also can't ever remember if the past tense of "lead" is spelled "lead" or "led.") Are there words you love? Are there slang words that you think are wonderful? Are there words that you just hate, for no apparent reason? (I refuse to use the words "paradigm" and "methodology." I can't stand them.)

Try talking with your students about words. Share some of your own opinions with them. Invite them to share their own opinions and observations. Then ask them to pay attention—really pay attention—to words for at least two weeks, collecting words for your own "M"-ey awards ceremony. (See student directions page 41.)

The exercise is interesting and enjoyable and also encourages students to pay attention to words. It helps them focus on the richness and potential and power of the English language. It's a great lead-in for vocabulary study.

The "M"-ey Awards

Words You Love

Words are everywhere. They are so common that sometimes we take them for granted. It's time to put them on stage, turn on the lights, and let them take a bow. It's time for the "M"-ey Awards.

Fill in your nominations for the categories below. You may nominate up to 10 words in any single category, and you may also add additional categories that you think deserve recognition. You don't have to nominate words for each category, but be sure to nominate at least 50 words, total.

1. Prettiest word (Examples: *gazelle, twilight*)

2. Ugliest word (Examples: *scarf, mucus*)

3. Silliest-sounding word (Examples: *bubble, squirt*)

4. "Surely that's not a word!" word (Examples: *flibbertigibbet, lollapalooza*)

5. Most "whispery" word (Examples: *powdery, silver*)

6. Word with the most terrible spelling (Examples: *hors d'oeuvres, cologne*)

7. Best sound-effect word (Examples: *thud, crunchy*)

8. Grossest-sounding word (Examples: *phlegm, goiter*)

9. Most official-sounding word (Examples: *plutocracy, subsidy*)

10. Most techno-sounding word (Examples: *gigabyte, Ethernet*)

11. Scariest-sounding word (Examples: *phlebotomy, ominous*)

12. Best tongue-twister word (Examples: *parallelogram, linoleum*)

13. Cutest word (Examples: *bongo, muffin*)

14. Most abrupt word (Examples: *flog, smudge*)

15. Best rhyming word (Examples: *humdrum, ringing*)

16. Fill in your own category here:

17. Fill in your own category here:

18. Fill in your own category here:

19. Fill in your own category here:

20. Fill in your own category here:

Kerfuffle

C. M. Thurston

As we struggle with all the demands made on us as teachers, it's easy to forget an important part of teaching English: having fun with words. Playing, fiddling, and noodling around with language can help students tune in to the power of words—an important step in learning to use language more effectively. Here are two exercises you might try.

Kerfuffle. I recently read *The Power of One* and discovered the word *kerfuffle*. It's my new favorite word. The author of the book, Bryce Courtenay, frequently uses the word to describe a small uproar or bit of confusion, as in "quite a kerfuffle among the fans." According to one dictionary, *kerfuffle* is more commonly used in British forms of English, but I think we should latch on to it on this side of the ocean and popularize it here as well. It sounds like what it means and has a certain bouncy flair. A riot is something to take seriously, but who could be very alarmed about anything called a *kerfuffle?*

Many words in our language have a certain weird charm, just because of the way they sound. *Flapdoodle* is a good example, or *willy-nilly, bamboozle,* or *blip.* One person may love the sound of the word *quintessential,* while *flibbertigibbet, plinth, lollygag,* or *malarkey* may appeal to another.

Try having your students page through dictionaries and, individually, find five words that they think have a great sound and might actually be useful to know. Ask them not to pick proper nouns because proper nouns have much more limited possibilities. (The word *Halmahera* may sound interesting, but how often are you ever going to need to refer to the largest of the Molucca Islands in Indonesia?) Have each student list his or her words and use each word in a sentence that shows its meaning.

Compile a list of all the words collected by students and share them with the class.

Muggles and gearheads. Many students have a vague notion that there is a giant master list of English words somewhere, a sort of dictionary for the universe. They don't understand that dictionaries reflect our language, rather than dictate it. New words are added to English constantly, and when a word appears frequently enough in books, magazines, or newspapers, a publisher will add it to its dictionary. Sometimes one publisher decides to add a word, while another publisher will decide not to add it. One dictionary might use a certain spelling, while another dictionary might use a different one. One might identify a word as slang, while another might not.

With the popularity of the Harry Potter books, *muggle* has become a widely-recognized new word. Here are a few more terms that are quickly becoming (or have already become) widely accepted and recognized: *bridezilla, gearhead, couch potato, tree hugger, granola head, jumping the shark.* (See www.wordspy.com for new words entering the English language.)

Ask your students to come up with a list of concepts, people or things that—as far as they know—don't have a word yet to describe them. Here are some ideas to get them started:

- People who try very hard to be funny but somehow just aren't.

- People who clearly smell of cigarette smoke but have no idea that they do.

- Children who refuse to eat anything green, like lettuce or peas.

- Teenagers who never respond when spoken to because they have on earbuds.

- Adults who say something and have no clue why kids are giggling. (An older teacher we know recently mentioned in passing that the first thing she did when she got home at night was slip on her thongs. When the kids started tittering, she was mystified. She finally realized she should have said *flip-flops.*)

- Text messaging while pretending to be doing something else.

- Shrinking a computer screen very quickly when you don't want someone to see what you were looking at.

- Girls who constantly flip their hair back, often in a flirtatious manner.

- The increasingly popular "talking in questions" style of speaking. (My dad? He's, like, having to commute an hour and a half to work each day? It's, like, causing some problems in my family? Like, I can't ever get him to pick me up after soccer practice? And my mom can't always get away until later?)

Compile a list and then have students come up with words they think describe the items listed. You might even want to create a matching "quiz" out of all the made-up words and their definitions, just for fun.

Fun with Writing

Writing Clearly

(Instead of "Utilizing the Skill of Written Communication to Obtain Prose That Is Easily Understood and Without Ambiguity")

Do you recognize the songs below? They are common tunes rewritten in very formal language.

Propel, propel, propel your craft,
Placidly down the liquid solution.
Ecstatically, ecstatically, ecstatically, ecstatically,
Existence is but an illusion.

Three sightless rodents, three sightless rodents.
Observe how they motivate, observe how they motivate.
They all motivated after the agriculturalist's spouse.
She removed their posterior extremities with a carving utensil.
Did you ever observe such a phenomenon in your existence,
As three sightless rodents, three sightless rodents?

The two songs are, of course, "Row, Row, Row Your Boat" and "Three Blind Mice." They certainly don't communicate nearly as well as the original songs!

Many people believe that their writing is better if they make it very formal, "fancy," or artificial-sounding. However, they are wrong. Good writing doesn't put on airs. It is clear and to the point.

In *The Elements of Style*, a classic book about writing, William Strunk, Jr., puts it this way:

> *Vigorous writing is concise. A sentence should contain no unnecessary words, a paragraph no unnecessary sentences, for the same reason that a drawing should have no unnecessary lines and a machine no unnecessary parts. This requires not that the writer make all his sentences short, or that he avoid all detail and treat his subjects only in outline, but that every word tell.*

(continued)

First, do it wrong. Just for the fun of it, see if you can do the opposite of what Strunk suggests. Choose any common song and rewrite it, using the most formal, artificial-sounding language you can. Use confusing words rather than clear ones. Make the song sound as complicated as possible. Then share your song with the class and see if anyone can recognize it.

If you can't think of a song, you might try one of these ideas: "Twinkle, Twinkle, Little Star"; "Jingle Bells"; "America the Beautiful"; the theme song for a television show; a commercial jingle; any popular song that most of the class would recognize.

Now, do it correctly. Clear writing sounds natural, not artificial. It is clear and contains no unnecessary "padding." As you may have noticed when you rewrote a song in the exercise above, short words are often clearer and more precise than long ones. Look at the examples below.

Complicated: The female propelled her right limb in a forward motion and made contact with her male companion's oral cavity, causing scarlet-hued liquid to issue forth in immense quantities.

Clear: She punched him in the mouth and he bled a lot.

Complicated: The young adolescent male entered the room used primarily for food preparation and placed himself before the refrigeration unit, which he proceeded to unshut. He established contact with a half-gallon of white, bovine liquid and also the right leg of a flightless fowl not known for its intelligence.

Clear: The teenage boy went into the kitchen, opened the refrigerator and grabbed a half-gallon of milk and a turkey drumstick.

Directions. Now rewrite the following sentences so that they are as clear as possible. Eliminate unnecessary words and substitute clear words for complicated, formal or artificial-sounding ones.

1. If we get to the essence of the matter, it could be said that I do not find her personality to be one that appeals to me or, for that matter, to be one which I can even tolerate.

2. The basic, fundamental truth is that a certain adolescent boy I observed caused me to conclude that this particular boy was what I would define as, at this point in time at least, very attractive, causing me to desire to approach him and make an introduction of myself, thus, hopefully, enabling myself to make his acquaintance.

3. The most authoritative administrator in the public educational institution issued a directive via the school-wide auditory electronic system. He stated that all adolescents in the institution were to cease and desist the practice of moving at a fast, springing gait toward the facility used for dining at midday.

Now read the long, wordy paragraph called "The Party," below. Then rewrite it, giving the same information, but in a clearer, natural-sounding way. The paragraph now contains 161 words. You should be able to condense it to under 60 or 70—or even as few as 49!

The Party

It was quite apparent that the party being held in the garage was, as a whole, noisy to a very great degree. Music that can only be described as loud came from the windows of the garage where the party was being held. The sum total of the teenage males and females in attendance made loud shrieking noises and engaged, together, in the act, or rather acts, of throwing cylindrical paper containers full of carbonated soft drinks at one another, along with spoonfuls of a substance used for dipping thin slices of fried potato. It is a fact that, in the middle of all this, an elderly neighbor woman, who was very advanced in age when compared with the boys and girls at the party, looked inside the garage and gasped, terribly shocked by the scene that she viewed before her eyes. She emitted a high-pitched sound that was loud and then lost consciousness on the paved entryway to the garage.

S-S-S-S-S-Secret Message

You are a secret agent in a foreign country, working closely with another agent. The two of you have agreed upon a code to be used in case of emergency. The code is as follows:

- If a message does not contain the letter *s* the receiver is in serious danger and should make plans to leave the city.

- If the message is less than 60 words long, the receiver should leave the city within 48 hours. If the message is between 60 and 70 words long, the receiver should leave within 24 hours. If the message is more than 70 words long, the receiver should leave immediately.

- If the sender believes the safest exit for the receiver is by boat, the message should contain three and only three words beginning with the letter *b*. If the safest exit is by car, the message should contain three and only three words beginning with *c*. If the safest exit is by plane, the message should contain three and only three words beginning with *p*.

- If the message is about a birthday party, the receiver should dress informally in comfortable clothes and sneakers as he flees the city. If the message is about an illness in the family, the receiver should dress in a business suit and carry a briefcase. If the message asks for a favor of some kind, the receiver should dress in a disguise.

You have just received word that your colleague is in danger and should leave, by boat, within 24 hours, dressed comfortably so that he or she can move quickly and easily if necessary. Using the code you have agreed upon, write a message that will safely convey the necessary information to your colleague.

Word Snapshots

The following assignment can be used in many different class settings. It is perfect to use as part of an autobiography unit in language arts. For those with a block program in their school, the assignment can be a cooperative effort, with English, social studies and/or art classes all involved. Word snapshots can also be used in a unit to enhance self-esteem, as a project for homeroom classes, or as a writing activity that is likely to get even reluctant writers to try to communicate, if only with a future version of themselves.

Getting started. Ask students to describe characteristics of a snapshot. Among other things, they are likely to mention that a snapshot "freezes" a moment in time. Explain that students are going to create snapshots that freeze time, but without using cameras or cell phones. They are going to create word snapshots that can be used in future years to give a more detailed picture of this particular period of their lives. Explain also that the snapshots have an added bonus: they make colorful, attractive posters to decorate their rooms, and many students may even want to make word snapshot posters as gifts for special friends.

Show students one girl's word poster, reproduced on page 55. Explain that this is a small poster, reproduced in black and white, instead of color, so it lacks the vibrancy of the original. Still, students should be able to get the idea. A word snapshot uses words to create a picture of a certain time in an individual's life. (Small graphics are allowed, but the word snapshot must communicate primarily with words.) When completed with care, the snapshots are attractive, fascinating keepsakes.

Show students also the selection from the sample explanation (page 53) that accompanies the sample word snapshot. The explanation is an essential part of the project. Why? Hard as it may be for students to believe, parts of their lives that are important today will not be important to them ten or fifteen years from now. Without the explanation, they are likely to look at their word snapshots in future years and wonder why in the world they included certain words and phrases. A color-coded key will also make it easy to distinguish different elements of the poster.

Materials. Collect a large number of thin, felt-tipped pens in as many colors as possible, and encourage students to bring in their own sets of pens as well. (Colored pencils can be used, but felt-tipped pens have more vivid colors, and students usually prefer them.) You will also need poster board. You may be able to provide poster board from school supplies, or you can encourage students to bring their own, especially if they want to use a special color or size. It's a good idea to encourage limiting the size of the posters. Half of a standard-sized piece of poster board works well. Larger sheets may be very difficult to fill, unless a student is particularly ambitious.

Making the posters. Have students spend some time alone and in groups, brainstorming categories they might include in their snapshots, as well as words and phrases that are important to them. Here are just a few ideas for categories to include:

Slang	*Hopes*	*Likes*
Dislikes	*Foods*	*TV Shows*
Fears	*Movies*	*People in the News*
Fashion	*Dreams*	*Incidents to Remember*

Before they begin work on their snapshots, suggest that students come up with a color code to distinguish items. (See sample explanation, page 53.) The codes can be complex or simple. One student used just two primary colors for his code: green for "good stuff" and blue for "bad stuff." He used other colors for graphics throughout the poster.

Explain that the posters are more interesting if a wide variety of lettering styles are used. Encourage students to bring in examples of lettering from magazines and newspapers and to print out samples of different fonts from a computer word processing program. There are an amazing number of styles that students can imitate.

Explain that goofs become a part of the design of a word snapshot. If someone ruins a letter, he or she might fill it in with color, change its shape and turn it into a simple graphic.

Many students start their snapshots with a word or phrase in the corner of the poster. Then they branch out from that first word, trying to make the poster as densely filled as possible. Another approach is to space key words and phrases all over the poster, going back later to fill in details and other words. Still another is to start from the center of the poster with a very important word, and work out toward the corners.

Writing the explanation. An important part of the word snapshot is the explanation to be included on the back of the poster. The explanation gives more information about words and phrases included on the snapshot. Remind students that the poster and the explanation should work together to help them re-create this time of their lives in future years. Perhaps their own teenage children will enjoy looking at the snapshots forty years from now!

(This may be one of those assignments that you don't choose to grade. If you feel you must, allow students to add explanations of the more private words and phrases after their posters are returned.)

Finishing up. Make arrangements for students to have their posters laminated, in order to preserve them, with their explanations on the back. Display the finished products around the room, or perhaps in a school display case. Then let the students take home the projects to enjoy in the weeks and perhaps months and years ahead.

My Word Snapshot for September 2, 2008

by Rachel Ortiz

In my word snapshot, "Obama vs. McCain" and other people in the news are written in blue. I'm excited about the election. Other people in the news include Hillary Clinton, Tiger Woods, the Dalai Lama, and one of my favorite musical groups, Rodrigo y Gabriela.

Things I really like are listed all over the poster in dark green. Here are a few of them:

- iPod—I love listening to all of my favorite bands wherever I go.
- text-messages—It's fun to instantly keep in touch with friends.
- animals—I love them because they are all so different and amazing.
- swimming—It has always been my favorite thing to do in the summer.

Things in lime green are my favorite foods. Here they are:

- banana split—I love this dessert because it has so many different flavors.
- pizza—I love it with anchovies!
- deep-fried shrimp—Who doesn't love it?
- chili—I love to eat it on cool fall days, but it's also good on hot dogs in the summer.

Recent movies I like are in black. Here are some of my favorites:

- *The Dark Knight*—This is an awesome movie!
- *Shrek 3*—I love Shrek, and this movie is as good as all the others.
- *Wall-E*—The story is really good and you fall in love with the robot immediately.
- *Indiana Jones and the Kingdom of the Crystal Skull*—I love Indiana Jones movies and this one ranks up there with the rest!

Things in pink are the things I dream of. Here they are:

- a new car—I would love to have a four-wheel-drive hybrid truck some day.
- lots of pets—I would love to have a place in the country so I can adopt tons of animals from the Humane Society.
- a trip to Hawaii—It is one of the most beautiful places on Earth and I've always wanted to go there.

Things in teal are my hopes:
- justice for all—It would be nice if this could happen someday.
- world peace—One day I hope there are no more wars.
- a job I love—I would love to have a job that puts a smile on my face every day.
- to be a good cook—I love to cook, but I need more practice.

Things in orange are my fears:
- spiders—They are creepy and crawly and they freak me out!
- war—People should think about it a lot more carefully before they do it.
- mean people—I don't like to deal with people who are rude and mean.

Things in red are my dislikes:
- cold—I like fall, but I hate winter!
- smog—It's unhealthy and it looks ugly.
- pickled herring—My mom always serves this at holidays and it is totally gross!

Things in lavender are some of my favorite text message and email abbreviations:
- LOL (laughing out loud)—I use this one a lot because my friends are funny.
- BFF (best friends forever)—I use this with my best friend, Alicia.
- TBC (to be continued)—This one's great for when you're interrupted by your mom to come and do your chores.
- WAYD (what are you doing?)—I use this all the time to catch up with friends.

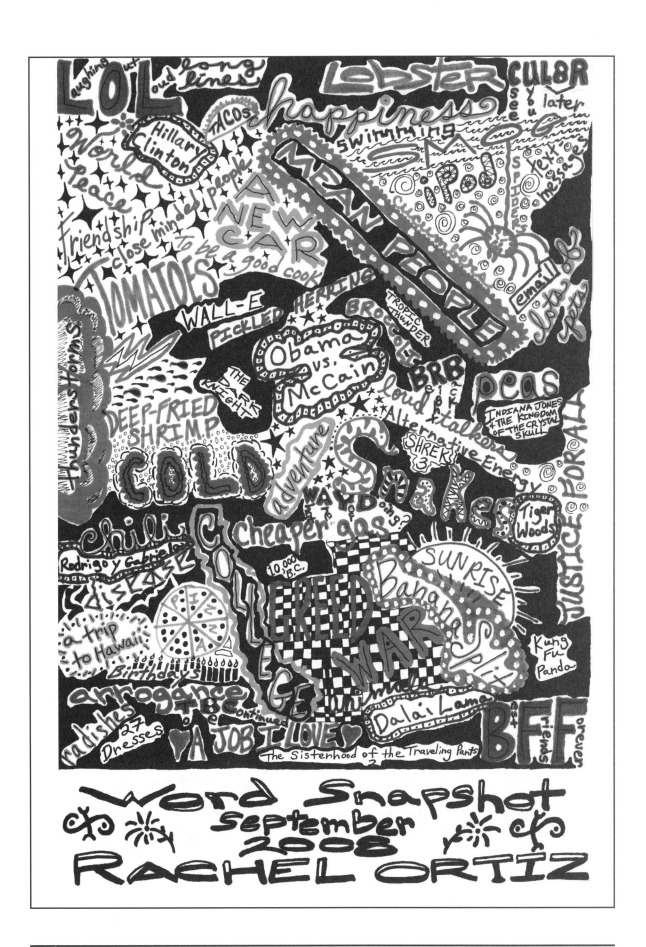

Be Specific #1

Your writing is much more effective when you use specific, interesting words—in other words, details. For example, here is a sentence that tells us something, but not much:

The cat got into the food.

Here is a sentence that gives us the same information, but in a much more interesting, informative way:

After Mrs. Donlan stepped into the laundry room, her cat Samantha sprang to the kitchen counter, stuck her nose in the butter dish, nibbled at the edge of the pork roast, tiptoed through the chocolate cream pie and sat contentedly beside the toaster, licking her paws.

Directions. Below is a bare-bones story—a story with only basic information. Rewrite the story, keeping the same essential facts but adding details to make it more interesting.

The boys and girls were watching television. It was late at night. It was stormy. There was a sound at the door. It frightened the boys and girls. Someone finally went to the door and opened it. The boys and girls screamed.

Getting started. Before you begin to write, think about the kind of story you want to create. Here are some questions you might want to consider: How old were the boys and girls? Where were they watching television? What were they watching? What kind of storm was it? What kind of sound was at the door? What did the boys and girls say when they heard it? How did they act? Who went to the door? Who—or what—was at the door? Why did everyone scream? What happened next?

After you have written a rough draft, exchange your paper with someone else in class. See if you can underline three places where the author could use more details. For example, if the author has written "little girl," you might underline that. Why? It could be changed easily to something more detailed and interesting, like this: toddler with shiny black pigtails, tied with pink ribbons.

After discussing your paper with your partner, see if you can add more details to your story. Then write your final draft.

Be Specific #2

Your writing is much more effective when you use specific, interesting words—in other words, details. For example, here is a sentence that tells us something, but not much:

The father spoke to his son.

Here is a sentence that gives us the same information, but in a much more interesting, informative way:

As Craig tiptoed into his home at 3:00 a.m., carrying his shoes and shutting the door softly behind him, he heard his father's cold "Good morning" come from the darkened living room.

Directions. Below is a bare-bones story—a story with only basic information. Rewrite the story, keeping the same essential facts, but adding details to make it interesting.

A car pulled up in front of the building. Someone watched as the driver got out of the car. There was a conversation. Then the car left.

Getting started. Think about the kind of story you want to create. What kind of car pulled up in front of the building? What kind of building was it? Who was driving the car—a male or a female? How old was the person? Did the person "fit" the kind of car he or she was driving? Who was watching? Did the person expect to see the driver? What did the people talk about? Who left in the car? Choose details carefully to create a story that will interest other readers.

After you have written a rough draft, go back and see if you can change some words to more interesting ones. For example, could you change the word *house* to *shack* or *mansion* or *condominium*? Could you change *spoke* to *whispered*, or *bright* to *blood red*? Could you change *walked* to *ambled*, *scurried* or *tiptoed*? Be careful to choose the most interesting, specific words possible for your story.

Write your final draft.

Groans and Grins

Groans

What are the little things in life that make you groan? In other words, what drives you crazy? Do not think about major problems like divorce, poverty, or bubonic plague. Instead, focus on the irritations in your life, the tiny, annoying things that just bug you to death. Write your "groans" in the form of a list. Here are a couple of examples:

- finding that my mom washed the jeans with my math homework folded up in the pocket
- trying to take a test while sitting by someone who has a runny nose and no tissue

Getting started. Sometimes it's hard to think of things that bother us, until we encounter them. To help you think, take a few minutes and imagine yourself going through a typical day. Think about your alarm going off, brushing your teeth, eating your breakfast, going to your locker, etc. Jot down any irritations you think of as you review your day. Then share some of the items on your list with others in a small group, and listen to their ideas as well. Sometimes listening to others can help you think of more ideas of your own.

It's also a good idea to brainstorm with members of your family for ideas. Family members can remind you of things you have complained about in the past.

Think about this assignment overnight, paying attention to little annoyances that may occur. Jot them down before you forget them.

Grins

Now, let's be more positive. What are the little things in life that make you grin? Don't think about major causes for joy, like falling in love, winning the lottery, or finding out school has been cancelled for the year. Instead, think about those little things that make you smile inside and make you feel good. Write your "grins" in the form of a list, following any special instructions your teacher may give you. Here are a couple of examples:

- when the most popular person in school smiles at me and remembers my name
- when my aunt sends me $20.00 instead of underwear for my birthday

Getting started. Follow the same approach as with "Groans," this time paying attention to things that make you grin, rather than things that make you groan.

Mythological Monsters

Today, nearly everyone has heard of monsters like Bigfoot, King Kong, Godzilla and the Loch Ness monster. Throughout history, monsters of many types have existed in legend, mythology and literature.

Greek mythology is a particularly rich source of monsters and strange creatures. Using encyclopedias, mythology books, the Internet and other resources in your classroom or library, find out about some of these creatures, listed below. Write a short description of each creature.

1. Argus
2. Cyclops
3. Chimera
4. Centaur
5. Cerberus
6. Gorgons
7. Griffin
8. Hydra
9. Harpies
10. Minotaur
11. Pegasus
12. Phoenix
13. Sirens
14. Sphinx
15. Titans

Create and write. Choose any two of the creatures listed. Using characteristics from each, create a new creature that is a combination of both. You may also want to add some new traits as well. Give the creature a name and write a short description of it. What does it look like? What are its "talents"? What makes it unusual? If you like, draw a picture to go along with your description. You may even want to write a myth of your own, based upon the new creature you have created.

Good, Clean Slang

Are your students clearly in need of a change of pace? You might try having your class take a look at slang. Slang is, after all, a real and important part of our language, a part that is often ignored in English classrooms.

One interesting class project is to produce a dictionary of good, clean slang. For how to go about it, see "Producing a Slang Dictionary" (below). "Slang Is Here to Stay" (pages 61-62) includes background material on slang for reading and discussion. "Making Your Slang Dictionary Entries" (63-64) includes step-by-step student instructions for writing dictionary entries, and "Say It in Slang" (page 65) is a composition assignment based on slang.

If you don't want to go to the trouble of producing a slang dictionary, you might want to use the background material for class discussion, followed by the composition assignment, "Say It in Slang."

Producing a Slang Dictionary

Collecting words. After the class reads and discusses "Slang Is Here to Stay," have the students start collecting slang terms. It's a good idea to collect the terms over a number of days, giving the students time to start paying attention to their language. You might want to spend a few minutes in class each day sharing terms. Students might begin by thinking of slang words for the following: *good, bad, food, great-looking, money, a child, braces, an adult, males, females, different, clothing items, computer terms, skateboarding, sports, music.*

Acknowledge that many slang words are related to sex, drugs and alcohol, but explain that this dictionary is not going to include those terms. The final dictionary will be called "Dictionary of Good, Clean Slang at (your school's name)."

Dividing the work. After the class has collected a large number of slang words, put the words on note cards or slips of paper and divide them among individuals or small groups. Go over "Making Your Slang Dictionary Entries" with the students, stressing that they should follow the step-by-step instructions as closely as possible.

Making the dictionary. After students have finished their dictionary entries, choose the entries to include in the final dictionary. Arrange them alphabetically, cutting and pasting from the student files. (You may have a student or an aide do this instead, of course.)

Add a cover (designed by a student), reproduce the completed pages, collate, staple and enjoy!

Slang Is Here to Stay

totally

ZIT

Most of us don't pay much attention to the words we use. Take a minute and think about all the words you use in a typical day—the questions you ask, the questions you answer, your conversations with friends, strangers, and family members. According to one language expert, 25% of all the words you speak in a typical day are one of the following nine words: *and, be, have, it, of, the, to, will* and *you.* Those nine words, plus an additional 34, probably make up 50% of all speech!

If you are an average American, you probably know from 10,000–20,000 words, many of which you don't use. About 10% of the words you know are slang words, and those are some of the words you probably use most.

What is slang?
Slang is hard to define. Generally, we can say that slang is an informal kind of language, more often spoken than written. Slang refers to words and phrases used in new or unusual ways. Slang words can be very expressive, funny and often offensive. Slang can refer to single words, like *geek,* or whole phrases, like *off-the-wall* or *chill out.*

Often, we aren't even aware that we are using slang when we speak. Slang changes so fast that it is sometimes hard to tell what is slang and what is not.

When is slang appropriate?
Slang definitely adds spice to our language, and even the most well-educated people have always used it at times—even Shakespeare. However, there are times when it is appropriate and times when it is not.

Let's suppose you have been invited to Washington by the president of the United States. As you sample the appetizers at a White House reception, the president approaches you. You say:

Dude! Whassup? Want a meatball? They're, like, soooooooo awesome. Seriously. **NOT!**

Of course it's unlikely you would speak that way at a formal reception. The informal language would be inappropriate there, though it might be perfectly acceptable at a party given by one of your friends. Generally, slang is considered inappropriate for formal speeches, business letters, most school work, and formal occasions.

Problems with slang.
Although slang definitely has its place in our language, its use can cause problems. For example, it can cause a loss of accuracy in communication. In some parts of the

like

---

country, parents are confused when they hear that their son or daughter is *going out* with someone, even though the two have never been anywhere together. The parents have difficulty understanding that *going out* can mean that two people just like each other.

Besides causing confusion, slang also sounds dated very quickly. Someone describing something as *groovy* or *psychedelic* would get strange looks today, even though those words were quite acceptable as slang forty years ago.

Can you think of some times when slang has caused confusion for you or someone you know?

Kinds of slang. Some slang words are new words. The slang word *ditz*, for example, is a word created to refer to a person who acts in a silly or brainless manner. The word has no other meaning in what we call standard English. *Scuzzy*, *nerd* and *zit* are other examples of slang words that have only slang meanings.

Some slang words, on the other hand, are old words which have new, slang meanings. *Hot* means "very warm" in standard English but something quite different when you talk about a *hot* guy or a *hot* girl. *Bananas* and *rip off* are other terms that have both standard English and slang meanings. *NERD*　*awesome*

The changing nature of slang. Most slang words are popular for a short time and then die out. In the late 1960s, it was a compliment to describe someone or something as *tough*, at least in some areas of the country. If a boy said, "She's a real tough girl," he probably meant that she was very attractive and he liked her. In the 1970s, *heavy* meant "excellent" or "wonderful." If someone said you were real *heavy*, it certainly didn't mean you should start worrying about your weight.

Some slang words eventually become standard English words, sometimes very quickly and sometimes after a number of years. *Hairdo*, *movie*, *soap opera*, *cab*, *phony* and *skyscraper* all began as slang words but are now considered standard English.

Some slang words stay around for a very long time yet never become standard. For example, *duds* and *booze* have been around for hundreds of years, yet they are still considered slang.

Why we use slang. Why do we use slang? Sometimes it's just habit. Have you ever noticed how often some people say *like* or *you know*? They sprinkle these words throughout every sentence yet aren't even aware they are doing so.

Sometimes we use slang just to be "in." Sometimes we use it because there is no standard word that means quite the same thing. Sometimes we use it because the slang words seem more expressive to us. Sometimes we use it just for fun.

Whatever the reasons we use slang, it is an important part of our language. Slang is definitely here to stay. *wow!*

Making Your Slang Dictionary Entries

Follow the step-by-step directions, below, to make your slang dictionary entries. Use reverse indentation, indenting all lines after the first. (See examples below.)

1. Write your first slang word or phrase, and make it bold.

    Example:
       bounce

2. Tell what part of speech the slang word usually is, using the proper abbreviation. Italicize the abbreviation.

    Example:
       bounce *v.*

    To help you, here is a list of the parts of speech, along with an example of each:

Part of Speech	Example	Abbreviation
verb	*ran (He ran.)*	*v.*
noun	*dog (Look at the dog.)*	*n.*
pronoun	*he, she (She is smart.)*	*pron.*
adjective	*pretty (She's a pretty girl.)*	*adj.*
adverb	*quickly (He ran quickly.)*	*adv.*
preposition	*of, on (He is on the roof.)*	*prep.*
conjunction	*and (She is pretty and smart.)*	*conj.*
interjection	*Oh! Wow! (Wow! Watch him run!)*	*interj.*

3. Tell what the word usually means, as clearly as you can.

    Example:
       bounce *v.* To leave or go away.

(continued)

4. See if you can think of a synonym for the word. Then write the synonym in capital letters. followed by a period. (Skip this if you absolutely can't think of a synonym.)

    Example:

    bounce *v.* To leave or go away. DEPART.

5. Write a sentence showing how the slang term can be used. Make your sentence as interesting as you can. Put it in italics.

    Example:

    bounce *v.* To leave or go away. DEPART. *When Felix got tired of the party, he said, "Let's bounce."*

7. If possible, add an illustration to help demonstrate the meaning of the slang term.

    Example:

    bounce *v.* To leave or go away. DEPART. *When Felix got tired of the party, he said, "Let's bounce."*

Say It in Slang

"The Emperor's New Clothes" is a fairy tale written by Hans Christian Andersen and first published in 1837. Here is a version written in the kind of slang popular in the late sixties and early seventies.

The Emperor's New Clothes

Once upon a time this real cool dude, who was the head honcho of this kingdom, had a real thing about his threads. The dude really grooved on wearing out-of-sight clothes. He spent a ton of time just changing his duds.

Well, one day these two guys blew into town. They said they were real pros at weaving and could weave real funky stuff, psychedelic stuff that was really out-of-sight. The thing was, the cloth really was out-of-sight to some people, or so they said. "Only people with a lot upstairs can see the beauty of our cloth," said the two guys. "Airheads can't. To anyone stupid, the cloth will be invisible."

The king got real hyped up and ordered some of the cloth for himself. The two guys got busy right off. First, they asked for bread to buy the finest silk and gold thread. The king gave it to them, but instead of buying thread, they slipped the dough into their backpacks. Then they pretended to weave, standing by the spinning wheels and pulling imaginary thread through the air.

The king kept sending his aides to check out the guys and see what they were doing. Each aide stuck his nose in and was freaked out to see nothing. Not wanting anyone to think he was a space case, each aide went back to the king and lied. "The stuff's really far-out," each reported.

Finally the king decided to bop on over and see for himself. "Dig it?" smiled one of the weavers. "Isn't it out-of-sight?"

"Yessssssssss," said the king, who was really flipping out. He took a deep breath to calm himself and said, "I mean, well, of course! It's heavy stuff! Boss! Real nifty! I want you to make me some new threads out of it right away. Then I can wear them in the parade day after tomorrow."

"No sweat," said the weavers. "We'll need more bread, and then we'll get right on it."

(continued)

Ideas That Really Work! • Copyright © 2009 Cottonwood Press, Inc. • 800-864-4297 • www.cottonwoodpress.com

The king gave them more cash, which they again stuck in their packs. They began pretending to cut and sew the invisible cloth. They really got into it, putting on quite a show. At last, they said they were ready and called the king.

"I can't believe these clothes!" cried the king. "I love them!" Of course he was lying. He couldn't even see them. Still, he nervously stripped down to his skivvies and let the weavers pretend to dress him in the new duds.

When the people saw the king parading down the street in nothing but his undies, they freaked. They didn't want anyone to think they were stupid, so they clapped and cheered and said, "Far out! Right on! Groovy! Out-of-sight!" The king smiled proudly, happy to see what sharp subjects he had.

But at last one little squirt turned to his father and said very loudly, "Hey, Dad. That guy ain't got nothin' on!" Everyone was shocked, but they knew this little kid wasn't stupid. After all, he was the only first grader in the kingdom to have a perfect report card. Everyone began whispering, repeating what the kid had said. Soon everyone was shouting, "The king ain't got nothin' on!"

The king turned bright red, from head to toe. At last he saw that he had been ripped off. The two weaving dudes split and lived happily ever after.

Find out how a fairy tale might sound in today's slang. Using any kind of modern-day slang (of the good, clean variety), write your own slang version of a popular fairy tale and share it with the class. Here are a few of the fairy tales you might consider rewriting: "Hansel and Gretel," "Rapunzel," "Little Red Riding Hood," "Sleeping Beauty," "Three Billy Goats Gruff," "Cinderella," "Snow White and the Seven Dwarfs," "Rumpelstiltskin."

Review the fairy tale you have chosen by recalling it with other class members or checking in a book of fairy tales. Then write your first draft, including as much slang as you can in your story.

Twenty-Five Words or Less

Contest instructions often begin with the words, "In twenty-five words or less…" For example, the Acme Company might ask, "In twenty-five words or less, explain why you use Acme's Acne-B-Gone Pimple Cream."

When you have only twenty-five words to explain or describe, you must choose your words very carefully. Try your hand at creating short, but vivid, word pictures. In twenty-five words or less, describe each of the following:

- something frightening

- something beautiful

- something disgusting

Remember: You have only twenty-five words for each description. Choose your words carefully and try to make each word contribute to the overall image you are creating.

One Syllable Challenge

People who want their writing to be clear and easily understood often choose short words over long ones. Instead of, "Joshua consumed a complete pizza and imbibed three beverages after the soccer competition," they might write, "Joshua ate a whole pizza and drank three Cokes after the soccer match."

Try your hand at choosing short, clear words. See if you can write an entire paragraph of at least five sentences, using only one-syllable words. Choose one of the following general topics:

- cats

- dogs

- food

- sports

- fish

- love

- hate

Toenails and Juice Boxes

When we think of poetry, we often think of "pretty stuff"—poems about love, beauty, flowers, sunsets, mountain peaks. Poetry, however, can really be about anything at all. Powerful poems have been written about a variety of things, including war, death, faces on the subway, a fly buzzing, something called a "Jabberwock," and a red wheelbarrow.

Write a poem about the goofiest, most unpoetic thing you can imagine—toenails, a juice box, a computer mouse, a baseball cap, a bottle of nail polish, a piece of dental floss, paper towels, etc. Use your imagination.

Start by jotting down everything you can think of about your subject. Then write a poem about your subject, using at least three of the features of poetry below.

Rhyme

Example:

> I think it's so neat
> That I've got such nice feet.

Metaphor

Example:

> Fido's brain was a black hole in outer space.

Simile

Example:

> His ears were like two large satellite dishes.

Personification

Example:

> The bottle cap wept as it was twisted away from its comfortable home on top of the plastic bottle.

Alliteration

Example:

> Betsy's Barbie doll baked on the big bureau by the bay window.

Ridiculous Similes

Similes compare two unlike things, using the words *like* or *as*. We're all familiar with common similes like "She was as beautiful as a rose," or "He was as tired as a dog," or "They were as scared as mice."

For a change, try writing similes that really stretch the imagination—similes that make ridiculous comparisons. For example, compare a person's voice and an egg. It's not easy to find a way to compare the two, but with a little imagination, it is possible. Here's one idea:

Her whiny, annoying voice melted all over me like a raw, runny egg yolk.

Now try writing similes that compare the following things:

1. a garbage disposal and a cloud

2. an iPod and spaghetti

3. a car and yogurt

4. a mountain climber and a piece of lint

5. a child and a toaster

6. a button and a lake

7. silence and a hamburger bun

8. a toothbrush and a sneaker

9. boredom and peanut butter

10. a lobster and a mop

Lessons in Writing

Be as Interesting as Possible

C.M. Thurston

For several years, I was part of a team of teachers who read and graded hundreds of writing samples by college freshmen. Our purpose was to determine whether each student should take a remedial writing course, a basic freshman composition course, or a more advanced writing course.

What is most memorable about the experience is how boring it was. The papers were, for the most part, excruciatingly dull. There was a sameness to them that made it hard to stay awake. Another grader and I soon found a way to break some of the monotony. I would read the first part of a sentence from a paper, and she would complete it—without seeing the paper. Then she would read the first part of a sentence from another paper, and I would complete it. What the students wrote was so similar from paper to paper that we could predict with great accuracy what they were going to say and how they were going to say it.

Now and then, however, a paper would perk us right up. The writing would make us laugh or bring us to tears. It would create a picture in our minds or help us see a point of view we had never considered. It would in some fundamental way get our attention with its originality.

That brings me to my point: Far too little time is spent helping students learn to be as interesting as possible in their writing. In my opinion, "Be interesting!" should be a classroom basic. No, it's not a basic that you will see in most lists of district or state standards. However, by teaching this basic, you will be helping students learn writing strategies that will help them become better writers—and, as a by-product, perform better on tests.

Here are just a few tips for helping students (or anyone else) make their work more interesting to readers:

- Use vivid verbs.
- Use details that appeal to the five senses.
- Avoid convoluted, confusing sentences that are difficult to understand.
- Quote what an authority has to say about a subject, or use the actual words of people involved in a situation or event.
- Leave out details and words that add nothing to the overall effect.
- Use anecdotes to illustrate a point.
- Use active voice, rather than passive voice.

Try using "The Candidate" (page 74) to give students practice with at least the first two items in the list above. (Some teachers may want to encourage students to try all strategies above.)

The Candidate

People running for political office don't have much of a chance if what they have to say puts people to sleep. The same goes for writers. They don't have much chance of communicating if what they write puts people to sleep.

Here are two easy ways to make your writing more interesting:

- Use vivid verbs. (The child *squirmed*. The dog *munched* on Cheetos. The biker *skidded* to a stop. The singer *waddled* over to the piano.)
- Use details that appeal to the five senses: sight, sound, taste, touch, smell. Here's one that uses all five:

As the smell of nail polish remover filled the cabin of the plane, the passengers glared at the woman sponging "Bubblegum Pink" off her fingernails. Her six-year-old sat next to her, whining, "I want a Coke! I want a Coke!" over and over and over again as he kicked the seat in front of him. As one more jab sent a sharp pain to his kidneys, the man in the seat yelped and stood up. He bumped the arm of the flight attendant, who spilled V-8 juice down his white shirt. The hungry woman sitting directly in front of the man didn't notice the commotion. She was groaning at the salty, cardboard taste of the free pretzels the flight attendant had handed out.

Here is a very boring account of a candidate's speech:

The candidate walked to the podium. The audience reacted. The candidate said something. The audience reacted again.

Using the basic facts, above, turn the paragraph into one that is interesting. Use interesting verbs and details that appeal to the five senses.

Explaining "Explain"

Students are always being asked to *explain*. Often, they don't do it very well. It's as if their eyes slide right over the word.

Sometimes, as teachers, we just assume too much. Perhaps students don't really know what it means to *explain*. Try a quick lesson in explaining.

Ask a question. Start by asking students a simple question that you know they can answer. Here are a few ideas:

- Is *American Idol* a good show?
- Should schools have dress codes?
- Should the driving age be raised?
- What is the worst show on television?
- What is the best movie you have seen lately?

When someone answers the question, say simply, "Explain." Here is an example of how the conversation might go:

> "Is *American Idol* a good show?"
> "Yes."
> "Explain."
> "It's fun to watch."
> "Explain."
> "I just did."
> "What makes it fun to watch?"
> "The people who are really bad."
> "Explain."
> "What do you mean?"
> "Why is it fun to watch people who are really bad? Can you give an example?"
> "Well, it's funny when people think they are so good, but they are really terrible.

You wonder how they ever got the idea that they were good. Like that guy who dressed up in the chicken costume and sang in that really high voice. It was fun to watch him act so serious when the audience was just cracking up. And then he got all mad and said things that got bleeped. Even his mom got in the picture and got bleeped, too."

> "What else makes it fun to watch?"

(continued)

"Well, it's because of the real people."

"Explain."

"Real people are on the show. Any normal person who can sing might try out and get on the show."

"Why does that make it fun to watch?"

"It's fun to imagine what it might be like to suddenly be famous and have everybody see you on TV. I mean, there are people watching all over America who actually *know* these people. My aunt lives on the same block as a guy who was on the show from California. And he even used to babysit for her kids."

"What's one more thing that makes the show fun to watch?"

"Paula Abdul and Simon Cowell."

"What about them?"

"Well, I just wait for Paula to say something kind of dumb. And Simon just says the *meanest* things."

"Why is *mean* fun to watch?"

"Well, what he says is mean in a funny way. It's like you just can't believe he said that. So you want to watch to see what he'll say next."

You might want to repeat the procedure with several students and several different questions. Then ask the class members to think about what they really did when they explained. After discussion, you are likely to end up with something like this:

Explain means...

- to give more information, usually by adding details and/or examples
- to say it another way
- to give reasons.

You might also alert students to a very practical fact of life: on tests and school assignments of any kind that include the word *explain*, more is almost always better than less. An *explain* instruction is looking for a lot of information, not a little.

Five minute exercise.
Ask students, in five minutes, to answer one of the following questions, or others more suitable for your particular students, on their own paper.

- What is one thing you like or dislike about the local mall? Explain.
- What is your favorite cartoon? Explain.

- What fast-food franchise makes the best hamburgers? Explain.
- What is the best video game you have played? Explain.
- What is the best sport to watch on TV? Explain.
- What makes *this* class the best one at school? Explain. (A smile helps here!)

Remind them to start by giving their answer in one complete sentence, then following up by giving more information. They might include details and examples that illustrate what they mean. They should also try restating their answer in a different way. (Example: I like the mall because the food court gives me a lot of choices. Restated: The food court lets me choose whatever I feel like eating, whenever I feel like eating it. I don't have to settle on one restaurant that might not have everything I want.)

Here is a sample paragraph. If you feel they need another example, share it with students as an example, before they write.

What I Like Best About the Mall

What I like best about the mall is the food court. With a food court, I get lots of choices. I can have a slice of pizza from Pizza Hut and a chicken sandwich from Chick-Fil-A and a Dilly Bar from Dairy Queen. I can eat whatever I feel like eating at a certain time. I don't have to settle on one restaurant that might not have everything I want. I don't have to be limited to what one restaurant has. The food court also is fun because you don't have to sit down and be quiet like you do in lots of restaurants. You can yell across the tables at your friends when you see them, and it's fine. No one is going to look at you weird or ask you to be quiet, like they would in a restaurant.

Have several students share their work. Then ask students to answer another *explain* question, perhaps related to something you have been studying in class, to turn in.

Teaching the Basics

What Is a Composition?

Students often know even less about writing compositions than we think they do. After assigning the first composition of the year, many teachers have been surprised to discover a student or two wondering, "What is a composition, anyway?"

It may be time to back up a bit. The lesson that follows (pages 79-84) gives students some very basic information about compositions. It then introduces students to a common type of composition, the five-paragraph essay.

It is important to stress that the five-paragraph essay is not the only form a composition can take. It is, however, an extremely useful form to learn, and one that can be varied for many purposes. Students who master the five-paragraph essay find it easier to manage the organization of any kind of paper.

The lesson below can be used in many ways. It can serve as an introduction for students who are learning to write five-paragraph essays or persuasive papers. For other students, it can help them understand that compositions have patterns of organization, that an effective essay generally makes a point, and that authors support their points with details, explanation and examples.

What Is a Composition?

You have written words. You have written sentences. You have written paragraphs. You have probably written letters and stories and reports.

But maybe you have not yet written a composition. Or maybe, if you have, you haven't really known what you were doing. You may have tried stringing a few paragraphs together and hoping for the best. You may even have resorted to copying a few paragraphs from the Internet—but let's hope not.

If you have been puzzled about compositions in the past, or if writing a composition is a new experience for you, don't worry. Writing a composition is not really such a difficult thing to do, particularly when you know more about how a composition is put together.

What is a composition? A composition is a paper written on a topic, a nonfiction topic. If you write a paper about your belief that we should spend more money on space exploration, your paper is a composition. However, if you make up a tale about the adventures of Glerpa, an alien from another galaxy who holds up a 7-Eleven store, then your paper is a story, not a composition.

What is a five-paragraph essay? A composition can have many patterns of organization, but a simple, basic pattern is the five-paragraph essay. This pattern is clear and easy-to-follow. After you learn it, you can adapt the pattern for many different purposes. You may even find that learning this pattern helps your organization in other areas, like making speeches or taking essay tests.

So what is a five-paragraph essay? It is simply a composition that makes a point. It does not wander here, there and everywhere. Instead, it makes a point and then sticks to backing that point. Furthermore, a five-paragraph essay will be—you guessed it—five paragraphs long.

How is a five-paragraph essay organized? A five-paragraph essay has three parts: an introduction, a body and a conclusion. The introduction tells us what you are going to say. The body says it. The conclusion reminds us of what you said.

If an essay has only three parts, why do we call it a five-paragraph essay? That's simple. The introduction and the conclusion are each one paragraph long. The body, however, has three paragraphs, each one giving support for the main point of the composition.

(continued)

You might picture the pattern of the five-paragraph essay like this:

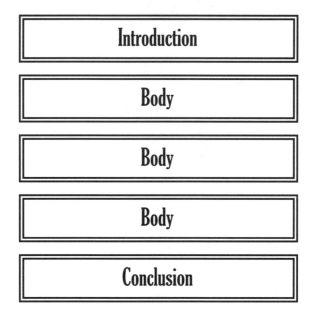

| Introduction |
| Body |
| Body |
| Body |
| Conclusion |

A look at a real-life situation. To help you see how an essay is organized, let's look at a real-life situation. Suppose that you have an 11:00 p.m. curfew, but you want your parents to let you stay out later on weekends. You approach them, whining, and say, "I want to stay out until 12:30 a.m. on weekends. You should let me!"

That is probably not going to convince them. Suppose, however, that you decide to use a five-paragraph essay to try to persuade them to change their minds. (All right, we know you wouldn't really write your parents a composition. We are supposing here, just for the sake of making a point.)

First, in your introduction, you would let your parents know what you want. You would want to be very sure they didn't misunderstand, as parents sometimes do. Therefore, you would be sure to state your overall point as clearly as possible.

Then, in the body of your paper, you would give three clear reasons for your point of view. Because parents aren't easily convinced, you wouldn't leave it at that. You would back up each of those reasons, using details, examples and further explanation. Each reason and its back-up material would be one paragraph long, making a body that is three paragraphs long, total.

Finally, to complete the body of your composition, you would write a conclusion. And what is the conclusion? It's the last chance you have to make your point. It is the place to pull together all you have said, leaving no doubt in your parents' minds that you are absolutely right.

On the next page is an example of a five-paragraph essay written to convince a boy's parents to change his curfew. Then there is a five-paragraph essay that discusses the value of cats over dogs. See if you can recognize all the parts of a five-paragraph essay in both compositions.

Moving My Curfew

Five-Paragraph Essay Example #1

For some time now, I have had an 11 p.m. curfew, even on weekends. When I was younger, this curfew was fine, and I didn't really complain. But now I have reached an age when this curfew is no longer suitable. For several reasons, it is clearly time to move my curfew to 12:30 a.m. on weekends.

First of all, I am growing up, and I'm soon going to be an adult. Like all teenagers, I need practice handling the greater freedom that goes along with being an adult. When teenagers don't get practice handling freedom, they often make many serious mistakes. For example, some teenagers go away to college and suddenly find themselves with a lot of freedom they aren't used to. They don't know how to handle it, and they get into trouble—partying too much, neglecting school work, sometimes even breaking the law. I believe it is better to increase freedom gradually, while a boy or girl is still living at home. That way the teenager learns how to handle freedom responsibly. I am ready to handle the freedom of a later curfew, and I believe I could handle it without making serious mistakes in judgment.

A later curfew is also important to me because I'm an active student. As you know, I take part in many extra-curricular activities, and many of these activities do not end until midnight. Because of my present curfew, I have to leave school functions over an hour before they are over. This is embarrassing and unfair, especially because I am often on the committee in charge of running these activities. Other students must take over for me when I leave. It also makes my friends think my parents don't trust me. I know that isn't true, but I can see why they would think that. A 12:30 curfew would allow me to stay until the end of school functions and give me enough time to get home without rushing.

Finally, I am a teenager who can be trusted to handle a 12:30 a.m. curfew. I know that many teenagers cannot handle much responsibility. Give them more freedom, and they are likely to get into trouble. However, I am clearly not that kind of teenager. I have proven myself to be a very responsible person. For example, I have never been in serious trouble, either at school or in the community. I also hold a part-time job and still manage to maintain a "B" average in school. And finally, when it's my turn to cook dinner at home, I always remember to do it and have it on the table on time. In other words, I am a person who uses my time wisely, meets responsibilities and stays out of trouble. It is quite reasonable to expect that I can be trusted not to abuse the privilege of coming home by 12:30 on weekends.

It is clear that my curfew should be moved to 12:30. I need the added freedom. I need to participate fully in extracurricular activities. I need your trust. I hope you will act right away to change my curfew. There is every reason to believe that I can handle the change in a responsible manner. Why not give me a chance to prove it?

Doug Matthew

Moving My Curfew

Questions

1. What is the author's overall point? State it in a complete sentence. (Note: If you want to impress someone, refer to the overall point as a *thesis* or a *thesis statement*.)

    _____

    _____

    _____

2. What are the three main reasons the author gives to support his overall point or argument?

    _____

    _____

    _____

    _____

3. In the second paragraph, the author uses an example to support his reason for needing a later curfew. What is the example?

    _____

    _____

4. In the third paragraph, the author uses two details to explain why he shouldn't have to leave school functions early. What are these details?

    _____

    _____

5. In the fourth paragraph, the author lists three examples to show that he is a responsible person. What are these examples?

    _____

    _____

    _____

    _____

6. In the conclusion, the author makes his main point again. What sentence sums up his point?

    _____

    _____

I'll Take a Cat

Five-Paragraph Essay Example #2

We were broke. I had just cooked a roast, a big pork roast that was supposed to last for the three evening meals remaining until payday. I put the roast on the table and went into the living room to get my husband. Then I stared in horror as our dog Daisy ran past us with the whole pork roast in her mouth. Perhaps that incident prejudiced me, but I know that a dog isn't the easiest animal in the world to live with. A cat, which can't even get a pork roast in its mouth, is a much better choice for anyone thinking about getting a pet.

In the first place, a cat simply can't make as much of a mess as a dog. Besides pork roasts, dogs chew anything they can get ahold of—socks, blankets, table legs, books, new leather boots and term papers due tomorrow. Cats chew nothing but their dinners. Dogs are also a mess, literally, to housebreak. They require weeks of newspapers spread out all over the kitchen and weeks of cleaning up endless "mistakes." With cats, all you do is put out a litter box, show it to the cat, and that's that. Let a dog in out of the rain and it will gallop through the house with muddy feet. Let a cat in and it will patiently lick itself clean before going anywhere. A cat simply disdains filth. It is much easier than a dog on both your home and your nerves.

Cats are also more suitable for urban life than dogs. Dogs have to be walked. They bark and drive the neighbors crazy. They crawl under the fence and roam over the neighbors' yards, munching the tomatoes in their gardens and leaving little piles beside their front steps. They break into garbage cans and run around with empty soup cans stuck on their noses—after spreading garbage from one end of the block to the other. Cats, however, walk themselves. You don't have to fence them in. They can be trusted. Let a cat outside and it will stroll politely through the neighborhood, bothering no one, except perhaps for an occasional dog that has crawled under a fence.

I admit that cats and dogs are both affectionate animals. However, a cat's love is easier to take than a dog's. Dogs shower you with attention, and there is something enormously appealing about a puppy jumping happily about and wagging its tail to greet you. But it is not so appealing to have the puppy ruin your new tights when it jumps on you. Nor do most of us enjoy the wet, slobbery kisses that dogs bestow upon us. A cat is more refined. Instead of jumping and slobbering, it daintily climbs into your lap and cuddles up, purring contentedly. Or it rubs softly against your legs, showing you, gently, that it cares.

To be fair, I must admit that my cat once walked through a chocolate cream pie I had sitting on the counter. But who's perfect? I can afford to replace a pie now and then, just for the pleasure of having a cat around. Dogs...well, they do have their charms. But when compared to cats, they come up losers in the pet department.

Susan K. Field

I'll Take a Cat

Questions

1. What is the author's overall point? State it in a complete sentence.

   _____

   _____

   _____

2. What are the three main reasons the author gives to support her main point?

   _____

   _____

   _____

   _____

   _____

3. What examples does the author give to support each of her three reasons?

   _____

   _____

   _____

   _____

   _____

4. What sentence in the conclusion restates the main point?

   _____

   _____

   _____

Writing an Introduction

The introduction is a very important part of reports, essays, compositions, articles, speeches and other forms of communication. It prepares us for what is coming up. It leads us into the subject matter at hand.

You may know that introductions are important, but you probably have trouble writing them. Most people do. Some people cope by writing the introduction last, after they have written the rest of the paper. That makes it easier for them to get started. Other people wouldn't dream of writing a paper until the introduction is written. Writing the introduction helps them organize their thinking, making the rest of the paper easier to write. Still other people write a very rough introduction first, coming back to it for more work after the paper is written.

Unfortunately, there is no magic formula for writing an introduction. Different papers need different kinds of introductions. Different people approach writing introductions in different ways. Sometimes, especially when you aren't very experienced at writing introductions, it helps to have some examples or models to follow. That doesn't mean you should imitate them exactly. It means you should use them for ideas, ideas you can adapt for your own work. Below are ideas for seven kinds of introductions. Try using one of the ideas for the paper or speech you are working on now.

The attention-getter. One effective type of introduction grabs the interest of your audience with an attention-getter. What is an attention-getter? It is just what it says it is: something that gets the reader's attention.

The attention-getter might be a startling statistic. It might be an interesting fact or a surprising statement. It might be a fascinating (and relevant) piece of trivia. A quick trip to the library or a search on the Internet can be a great help in coming up with information for an attention-getting introduction.

Here's an example of an introduction that uses an attention-getter:

> *You may not realize it, but you share your birthday with at least nine million other people. Nine million people were born on the same day you were, and nine million people could be celebrating their "special" day at the same time you are. Although our birthdays may not be unique, the way we celebrate them can be. For example, whenever anyone in my family has a birthday, we do some strange things. I'll bet there isn't one single family on earth who celebrates birthdays quite the way we do.*

(continued)

Quotations. Another way to begin an introduction is with a quotation. The quotation could be from a famous person or a leading authority on your subject. It could be from an ordinary person who has said something particularly interesting or colorful about your topic. It could be from a character in a movie or a book. It could be from a newspaper editorial or a magazine story. It could be from just about anywhere, as long as the quotation is related to your topic. It also helps if the quotation is particularly clever, humorous, interesting, or wise.

In general, it is *not* a good idea to start out by saying, "According to Webster's Dictionary..." That kind of quotation has been overused, and it is not usually very interesting.

Here's an example of an introduction that uses a quotation by a well-known person:

> *The great jazz musician Eubie Blake said on his 101st birthday, "If I'd known I was going to live this long, I'd have taken better care of myself." Blake had the right idea, even if it was a little late. We should take care of ourselves, and one of the best ways is with regular exercise. For both children and adults, one of the best exercises is one of the easiest and least expensive–plain old walking.*

Here is an example of an introduction that uses a quotation by an ordinary person:

> *"I hate kids," my Uncle Dave always said when he came to visit. "I don't know why on earth anyone would have them." His voice was gruff and he didn't smile when he said it. But he always said it while bouncing my little sister on his knee, or slipping my brother a candy bar, or handing me a new comic book. Uncle Dave was a man with a tough outside but a gentle inside.*

An anecdote. Think about the way you sometimes tune out in class. The teacher will be talking on and on, and your mind will be far, far away. Then the teacher will say something like this: "It reminds me of the time I was in high school and we had this special dance where we..." Suddenly you will find yourself listening. That is because the teacher is telling an anecdote—an interesting personal story from his or her life. Because people tend to like anecdotes, using one can be an effective introduction for a speech or for a composition. Here's one example:

> *Last Tuesday I raced toward my math class, just as the bell was ringing. I had mustard on my hands, and I needed to go to the bathroom. My heart was pounding from my frantic rush down the hall to be on time, and I was so rushed I had grabbed the wrong notebook from my locker. I slid into class, only to run smack into my math teacher, knocking him flat. No, I am not an irresponsible guy trying to make up time I wasted during my lunch hour. I am the victim of a lunch period that is far too short for a student's needs.*

A list or series. Sometimes you can use a series or a list to introduce a subject. The list might take the form of several interesting figures, a number of facts, or a series of examples related to the subject of your paper. Here is an example:

Bob eats only at restaurants with pictures on the menus. Sam always finds an excuse not to help his daughter with her homework. Linda turned down a promotion because her new responsibilities would include reading reports. Bob, Sam and Linda are among the growing number of adults in this country who can't read. The problem is becoming a serious one, and it's time we do something about it.

Present the problem. Another kind of introduction presents a problem and then proposes a solution. Here is an example:

One of the most serious problems to confront teenagers today is suicide. It is a problem that touches every teenager at some time or another. It is not a problem to be hushed up, whispered about, or ignored. By the time he or she graduates from high school, nearly every teenager will know at least one person who has attempted suicide, and a growing number of teenagers will have considered it themselves. The best way to help teenagers deal with suicide is to take it seriously.

Who-what-when-where-why-how. Sometimes a straightforward introduction is best, an introduction that gives just the facts. In this type of introduction the writer answers these basic questions: Who? What? When? Where? Why? How? Here is an example:

Last weekend, the Longview Lancers won a stunning victory over the crosstown rival, the Templeton Tigers, at the county basketball tournament. The Lancers won, largely because of the extraordinary agility of player Scott Girard.

Whatever kind of introduction you write, keep the following tips in mind:

- For most papers, it is best not to "announce" your subject.

  No: I am going to tell you about aardvarks...

  Yes: Aardvarks are interesting animals...

(continued)

- Don't *assume* that the reader knows what you are talking about. Be specific.

No:

The solution the principal proposed for the lunch hour problem is ridiculous. It is sure to...

Yes:

For the past few months, people who live near our school have been complaining about students leaving litter on the streets at lunchtime. Last week our principal announced a solution to that problem: students may no longer leave campus for lunch. That solution may solve the problem, but in the long run, it is not a very sensible solution at all. It is sure to...

- Don't use the title as part of your introduction. Begin your paper as if the title weren't there.

No:

Is There Life in Outer Space?

Many people think there is. Even some scientists are starting to think that chances are good. Someday, we may even...

Yes:

Is There Life in Outer Space?

Perhaps from the beginning of time, people have wondered if there could be life in outer space. Today, no one knows for sure, but many people believe there is. Even some scientists are starting to think that chances are good. Someday, we may even...

Introduction to Plenzenarks

Write six different introductions to a paper with this title:

Plenzenarks

What are plenzenarks? That's up to you. You can make up "facts" and use your imagination freely.

For each introduction, use one of the following approaches to writing an introduction:

- The attention-getter

- A quotation

- An anecdote

- A list or series

- Present the problem

- Who-what-when-where-why-how

Hector Hillerman's Favorite Things

A Lesson in Sorting, Selecting and Organizing Information

Inexperienced writers often have difficulty organizing their material. When they collect information for a report or a composition, they frequently toss the information onto the page, with little regard for form, organization or even relevance. It's almost as though—happy to have collected something—they are content simply to get it onto paper.

"Hector Hillerman's Favorite Things" is a five-part lesson that will help your students learn about sorting, selecting and organizing information.

Step one. To begin the lesson, pass out "Things About Me" (page 93) and have students complete the items. Encourage them to be as specific as possible, taking time to write thoughtful answers. (In fact, it's a good idea to let them finish the activity at home, perhaps even enlisting help from family members.) Because some of the material they write about will be shared with other class members, remind them not to include private information they would not want others to know about.

Step two. After students have completed "Things About Me," tell them that a mythical student, Hector Hillerman, has also completed the activity. Pass out "Things About Hector Hillerman" (page 94) and read it aloud with the class.

Then explain the assignment: Students are to write one paragraph about Hector, a paragraph introducing him. Because Hector's introduction is to be only one paragraph long, students won't be able to include every piece of information from "Things About Hector Hillerman." They will need to focus on one "thing" about Hector.

Ask students to look over the facts about Hector and to come up with ideas for an area of focus. Some possible ideas: humor in Hector's life, Hector's belief in working hard to get what he wants, Hector's hatred of algebra, Hector's love of swimming. Ask students, as a group, to agree upon one area of focus for the assignment.

Step three. Have students imagine that they can ask Hector some follow-up questions, to help with their paragraphs. What questions might they choose?

For example, if they have chosen "humor in Hector's life" as an area of focus, they might ask some of the following questions:

- When did you first become interested in Adam Sandler? Why?
- What do you like most about Eddie Murphy?

- What did you learn about joke-telling from your father?
- When was the first time you found out you could make people laugh? What happened?

To generate answers to the follow-up questions, try one of the following suggestions:

- Have class members take turns contributing answers for Hector.
- Have another teacher or student visit the class, playing Hector and answering questions.
- Answer the questions yourself, giving answers for Hector.

When the class has answers to their follow-up questions, have them add the answers to "Things About Hector Hillerman." Finally, have them write a topic sentence for a paragraph about Hector. Some possibilities:

- Hector Hillerman is a funny guy.
- Hector Hillerman's most important quality is his sense of humor.
- Hector Hillerman's dream is to become a comedian.

Step four. Now it's time to write. Have students, individually, write paragraphs about Hector Hillerman, using only "things" about him that are related to the topic sentence. Point out that much of the information on "Things About Hector Hillerman" will be irrelevant. Students will have to sift through the information, choosing only material that supports the topic sentence.

Have students read aloud their paragraphs, or reproduce several good examples. It's a good idea to write your own version, as well. Perhaps you might come up with something like this:

> *Life is not a bowl of cherries for Hector Hillerman. It's a barrel of laughs. Hector has what he believes is a great sense of humor. He learned to love comedy at an early age, probably because of a father who played practical jokes. One of Hector's first memories is of his father dressing up as a woman to be the blind date for a young bachelor friend, who didn't appreciate the joke. He also remembers laughing at his father's comical brother Clayton, who played the dwarf Dopey at Disneyland one summer. When Hector was ten, his Uncle Clayton gave him a DVD of an Adam Sandler movie, and soon Hector was imitating Sandler, reciting parts of the movie for his friends and making them laugh. Later he became an Eddie Murphy fan. He admired Murphy's ability to imitate people and to create interesting and funny characters. Someday Hector hopes to become a stand-up comedian as funny as both Sandler and Murphy. His dream is to do his routine on "The Tonight Show" and then sign a contract for a major motion picture.*

(continued)

Step five. Students now get a chance to write about people they know—fellow classmates. Have the students go over the "Things About Me" sheets completed earlier, seeing if they can add any more information. Then divide the class into pairs.

Explain that each student is to write a paragraph of introduction about his/her partner. Just as they did with Hector Hillerman, the students are to find a theme or area of concentration, write a topic sentence and ask follow-up questions to obtain more information before they begin writing.

As each student reads his or her finished introduction aloud, ask the class to listen for how well the student stayed focused. Each paragraph should contain only information that supports the topic sentence.

You might photocopy the entire collection of introductions, giving copies to the students. Or you might post the introductions on the bulletin board, along with snapshots or school photos of the students described.

Things About Me

Some things I have a lot of information about:

Not to brag, but three things I do well:

Some things I particularly value or cherish:

Something that bothers me (a question, a mystery, a problem):

Some things I oppose or reject:

Some unusual things that have happened to me:

Some unusual or interesting things I have seen:

Unusual things about my background (places I have lived or visited, experiences of family members, family history, etc.):

Something I daydream about:

Something I would do if I knew I had only one year to live:

Some things I have learned from important people in my life:

Something that recently made me happy:

Things About Hector Hillerman

Some things I have a lot of information about:

Swimming, Eddie Murphy, motorcycles, World War II airplanes.

Some things I particularly value or cherish:

My friends, my sense of humor, working hard to get what I want, my Adam Sandler autograph, my family.

Some things I oppose or reject:

Country music, people who are always putting down other people, algebra, quiet people—they make me nervous.

Some unusual or interesting things I have seen:

The inside of the baggage compartment on an airliner. A dead armadillo.

Some things I daydream about:

Winning a gold medal in swimming at the Olympics, becoming a successful comedian, getting rich, owning my own island, passing algebra.

Some things I have learned from important people in my life:

From my father, how to tell a good joke. From my mother, not giving up when I really want something. From my grandfather, looking at the positive side of things. From my fifth grade teacher, that I wasn't really stupid at math and I could learn long division. From my sister, that girls are impossible for boys to understand.

Not to brag, but three things I do well:

Swimming, making great green chile enchiladas, making people laugh.

Something that bothers me (a question, a mystery, a problem):

Why did my parents get divorced?

Some unusual things that have happened to me:

Broke my leg falling down the stairs while running away from a guy in my apartment who doesn't think water balloons are funny; got lost at Sea World when I was nine.

Unusual things about my background (places I have lived or visited, experiences of family members, family history, etc.):

My great-grandmother died a week after coming to America, leaving my great-grandfather with only $1.50 and an eight-month-old baby. He didn't even speak English. Still, he managed to survive and eventually started a restaurant in Boston that was very successful for 25 years. My mother can speak three languages. My uncle played the dwarf Dopey at Disneyland in the summer of 1986.

Something I would do if I knew I had only one year to live:

I'd travel all over the country on a motorcycle.

Something that recently made me happy:

Getting an "A" on the speech I gave, which was a funny talk about the miseries of wearing a cast on one leg. Also, getting a first place in the swim meet last week.

Plagiarism

C.M. Thurston

Plagiarism is widely misunderstood—by students, by parents, even by teachers. A friend of mine recently heard a woman defend her daughter, who had copied large segments of her term paper. "She copied the stuff herself," the woman said. "I thought plagiarism was when you didn't do your own work."

My brother, a high school biology teacher, has a problem with kids copying things off the Internet. "One student didn't even bother to retype what he found," he told me. "He just printed off what he found on the Internet, scrawled his name at the top, and handed it in. When I told him he was supposed to write a report in his own words, he looked baffled. 'Why?' he said, gesturing to his print-out from the Internet. 'It's all right there.'"

Another friend of mine talked to her eighth grader about plagiarism. "Do you know what it means?" she asked.

"Sure," he said. "It's when you copy out of the book."

"What about copying from the Internet?" she asked.

He looked puzzled. "I don't know." Like many people, he wrongly thought it was possible that the Internet just might be fair game.

Sometimes students don't understand *how* to put things in their own words. Sometimes they simply don't understand what plagiarism is. The following activities (pages 96-98) give students some guidelines to follow.

In Your Own Words

What does "In your own words" really mean? When you write a report on a subject for school, you are supposed to read about your subject and then put what you learn into your own words. Unfortunately, many students have some real misconceptions about what that means.

Don't just change a word here or there. Many students think that if they change one word in a sentence, they are not copying.

They are wrong. Just changing "laughed" to "giggled" in a sentence or paragraph, but leaving everything else the same, is copying. Putting things in your own words means that you change it substantially.

Don't use words if you don't know what they mean. Find out what they mean. Then explain things in words you do know and are used to using.

For example, imagine that you read a paragraph that mentions a *wizened* apple. You don't know what *wizened* means and have never used the word. When you put the material into your own words, you should not use *wizened* to describe the apple. After you look up the word and find out what it means, you might describe the apple as *wrinkled* or *shriveled up*.

Don't try to retell things sentence by sentence. Read several paragraphs. Or, if it's short, read the entire piece. Then put the original material aside and try to sum up what you just read, without looking at the original. You may even want to change the order of things entirely.

Keep it simple. Sometimes it helps to pretend you are telling a child what you just read. Try to explain things in words that the child would understand.

If you use quotations, give credit. Sometimes you may find that you just can't think of a way to restate a phrase or a sentence. You can copy it, if you put it in quotation marks and give credit to the source. For example, you might write something like this: *According to an article by Darren Rovell of ESPN.com, a two and a half minute Nike music-video-style basketball commercial has* "achieved cult proportions" *and is* "the rage in high schools and around the office water cooler."

Use direct quotations sparingly, however. Also avoid plopping a quotation into the middle of your work with no explanation. Instead, use words like "according to" to introduce the quotation and weave it into your own work.

Pick and choose what you think is important. When you reword something, remember that you shouldn't try to include everything from the original.

What Is Plagiarism?

In a junior high science classroom, a girl named Cheryl read aloud her report on pearls. The last words she read were, "Related articles in *World Book* include: Birthstone, Button, Carbonate, Conch, Gem (color picture), Mollusk, Oyster." Cheryl had copied her report, word for word, from the encyclopedia. She hadn't even paid enough attention to see that the last sentence was a dead giveaway.

Cheryl was guilty of plagiarism. What is plagiarism? It is a form of stealing. It is the stealing of another person's words or ideas and using them as your own. Cheryl had plagiarized her report because she had pretended the *World Book* article was her own work.

Plagiarism is a serious offense.
Plagiarism is against the law. Of course it is unlikely that the police are going to come into a school and arrest a boy or girl for plagiarism, even if the student is guilty. However, older students and adults who are caught plagiarizing can get into serious trouble—losing lawsuits, having their careers ruined, flunking courses, being expelled from school.

Give credit to your sources.
There is nothing wrong with using the words of another—if you give that person credit for the words. There are a number of ways to do that. The simplest way is just to say so. Tell who you are quoting, and then put quotation marks around the person's words.

What about changing a word here and there? Many students think that if you change "a" to "the" in a sentence, you aren't copying. Wrong. Even if you change several things slightly but leave the material essentially the same, you are still plagiarizing.

Plagiarism applies to ideas, as well as words.
Plagiarism can exist even if you don't copy at all! Using someone's ideas as your own is also plagiarism.

Suppose that a Dr. Joe Schmoe writes a newspaper article with a suggestion for improving the U.S. economy. He suggests that all students be required to drop out of school between the ages of 12 and 15, to save school districts money and to allow students more time to spend money at local malls. You think that sounds like a great idea, so you write an English paper suggesting the same thing but never mentioning Dr. Schmoe. Even if you don't use Dr. Schmoe's words, you have plagiarized his ideas.

The solution? You don't have to give up the idea for your English paper. All you have to do is summarize Dr. Schmoe's ideas, giving him credit for them. Then you can go on to discuss and expand on those ideas—in your own words.

Recognizing plagiarism.
Let's see if you can recognize plagiarism. Read the following paragraph from the book *Madonna*, by Jessica Maxwell (Turman Publishing Company; Seattle, 1987):

It's too easy to think that Madonna became a star overnight; she didn't. Madonna worked very, very hard for six long years before she got her first record deal. She was poor, and she lived in ratty old rooming houses in New York City. There were times when all she had to eat was popcorn. "I lived on popcorn," Madonna says. "That's why I still love it. Popcorn is cheap and it fills you up."

Now look at each of the following paragraphs from student reports on Madonna. Put a "P" beside each paragraph that includes plagiarized material, and be ready to explain what is wrong. Put an "OK" beside each paragraph that contains no plagiarism.

1. It's easy to think that Madonna became a star overnight, but she didn't. She worked very, very hard for six years before she got her first record deal.	
2. Madonna has worked hard to become a star. Things were hard for her when she was living in New York City, trying to get her first record deal. Sometimes she was so poor that she had nothing to eat but popcorn.	
3. Madonna used to be poor and lived in ratty old rooming houses in New York City. There were times all she had to eat was popcorn.	
4. Madonna is one of my favorite stars. Many people think she was an overnight success, but according to Jessica Maxwell in her book *Madonna*, Madonna "worked very, very hard for six long years before she got her first record deal."	
5. Madonna was very poor while she struggled to become a star. She used to live "in ratty old rooming houses in New York City. There were times when all she had to eat was popcorn" (Jessica Maxwell, *Madonna*, 1987).	
6. Madonna is strong. She worked very, very hard for six long years before she got her first record deal. It was hard for her. She was poor, and she lived in ratty old rooming houses in New York City. It must have been awful. There were times when all she had to eat was popcorn.	
7. "It's too easy to think that Madonna became a star overnight; she didn't. Madonna worked very, very hard for six long years before she got her first record deal. She was poor, and she lived in ratty old rooming houses in New York City. There were times when all she had to eat was popcorn. 'I lived on popcorn,' Madonna says. 'That's why I still love it. Popcorn is cheap and it fills you up.'"	

Parts of Speechless

If you have studied parts of speech, you know how important nouns and verbs are in our language. Now take a closer look at four other parts of speech—adjectives, pronouns, prepositions and conjunctions. See if you can complete the exercises below.

1. Write a paragraph that describes two children playing, but use no pronouns.

2. Write a paragraph about someone interacting with a pet, but use no adjectives, other than the articles *a, an* and *the.*

3. Write a paragraph describing a place where people normally eat meals, but use no prepositions.

4. Write a paragraph about two people involved in some kind of athletic event, but use no conjunctions.

5. What did you discover in writing the paragraphs above? Which task did you find most difficult? What conclusions can you make?

What's That Smell?

Writing with the Senses

The sense of smell is a powerful one. It can instantly transport a person to another place and time. Sometimes, it happens so quickly that the person doesn't even realize that it is a smell that has triggered the memory.

Here are just a few real-life examples:

The smell of frozen burritos cooking always reminds Samantha of the musical group Three Dog Night. Whenever her parents played golf, they picked up frozen burritos for supper. As the family waited for them to cook, they listened to music.

The smell of ammonia reminds Mike of chocolate chip ice cream. When he was very young, his family sometimes went to Wiswell's, an ice cream store that used ammonia for cleaning. One day when his mom took him for a treat, the smell was particularly bad. He ordered chocolate chip ice cream, got sick from the smell of the ammonia and promptly threw up all over the store.

The smell of Noxema skin cream reminds Stacy of her mother.

The smell of wet, stinky towels reminds Susan of a boy named Alan, who sat behind her in elementary school and, in her opinion, needed to take more baths.

What smells bring up memories for you? Take some time to think, discuss and share with others. Here are a few ideas to help you get started:

1. Think of food smells—bacon frying, hamburgers cooking on the grill, spoiled milk, fresh strawberries, steamed broccoli, homemade bread, etc.
2. Think of the smell of personal products—perfumes, soap, aftershave, hair spray, etc.
3. Think of outdoor smells—pine needles, smoke, car exhaust, gasoline, rain, wet dogs, etc.
4. Think of indoor smells—furniture polish, detergent, clean sheets, freshly-bathed babies, a kitchen garbage can, etc.
5. Think of school smells—gym lockers, chalk, bubblegum, tacos from the lunchroom, etc.

Now write a paragraph on the topic, "Where One Smell Takes Me." Describe the smell. Describe exactly where the smell "transports" you. What do you see? What do you hear? What do you feel? What do you taste? Use as many senses as possible to describe what happens in your mind when you experience this smell. Use details. Be specific.

Alphabet Adjectives

Write a story that uses adjectives that begin with all the letters of the alphabet, in order. After an adjective that begins with *a*, use an adjective that begins with *b*, then an adjective that begins with *c*, etc. (There can be other adjectives in between. In other words, your story can have more than 26 adjectives.)

For example, you might start a story like this:

> When <u>a</u>ngelic Marissa went to the <u>b</u>eauty shop to get a permanent that would make her hair <u>c</u>urly, she took along her <u>d</u>evoted dog, Dimples...

Be sure to underline the first letter of each alphabet adjective.

Verbs Rule!

"Groking" It

C.M. Thurston

There is a wonderful term in the book *Stranger in a Strange Land*, by Robert Heinlein. The term is *grok*. When Michael Valentine Smith, who was raised on Mars, *groks* something, he understands it fully, feels it, grasps it and all its layers of meaning. There is a difference between knowing something and "groking" it.

Here's an example. I grok an old movie called *Little Shop of Horrors*. I think it is absolutely brilliant on many levels and very funny. I love the music. I love the deliciously stupid story. When Steve Martin sings "I Am the Dentist," I absolutely crack up every time. Many people I respect, however, don't share my feelings. They see that the movie is a comedy. They see that it is a musical. They may even sort of like it. However, they just don't grok it.

Let me give another example. Something I do not grok is football. Though I vaguely understand the rules, the game to me is a maze of men in tight pants running around aimlessly for short periods of time in between long commercials. When my husband says, "Look at this amazing pass," I dutifully look. I understand that it is quite an amazing pass. I believe that it is quite an amazing pass. I just don't grok it. I will never grok it.

That brings me to the subject of sentence fragments. We tell students over and over, "Don't write sentence fragments. A complete sentence must have a subject and a verb." They know that. They have been told that year after year after year. The problem is that they don't really grok it. Here's one way to get them started on the path to groking.

Two-word sentences. Explain to students, again, that sentences must have a subject and a predicate. Then, to illustrate, strip things down to the basics, concentrating on two-word sentences that have only a subject and a predicate and nothing else. Show them this list of 10 two-word sentences:

1. Dogs bark.
2. Cats meow.
3. Parents yell.
4. Snakes slither.
5. Hamsters smell.
6. Bullies bully.
7. Commercials sell.
8. Babies burp.
9. Kids rule!
10. Dad snores.

Point out the nouns: *dogs, cats, parents, snakes*, etc. Point out the verbs: *bark, meow, yell, slither*, etc. Then have the class as a whole come up with ten more two-word sentences. (There is a 99% chance that "School sucks" will be one of the examples they come up with. To head them off, you may want to rule out *sucks* ahead of time.)

Finally, have them each write 25 two-word sentences of their own. Just for fun, if there is a holiday approaching, you may want them to limit their sentences to holiday related sentences. Other topics, of course, may work for other times of the year.

Writing a two-word sentence poem.
After students have their lists of 25 two-word sentences, have them pull samples from their lists into a poem based on a theme. (Of course, they can also add other sentences or alter their sentences to help with rhyming.) For example, a student might pull together some Halloween sentences into a poem made up of two-word sentences:

Witches cackle.
Goblins grin.
Bats swoop.
Heads spin.

On the topic of school, a student might write:

Books bore.
Teachers drone.
Time crawls.
Kids groan.

Testing whether or not they "grok" it.
After students have written their two-word sentences and their poems, show them the following two-word sets. Some of the sets are sentences. Some are not. Have students separate the sentences from the fragments.

1. Temperatures rise.
2. Book bag.
3. Bat wings.
4. Parents yell.
5. Girls giggle.
6. Boys' bathroom.
7. Snow falls.

8. Snow angel.
9. Noses twitch.
10. Eyes close.
11. New shoes.
12. Computers crash.
13. Photocopiers jam.
14. Storms rage.

15. Dangerous tornado.
16. Funny movie.
17. Parents listen.
18. Brothers fight.
19. Credits roll.
20. Good night.

By this time, they should be starting to grok a sentence. They should recognize the sound of a sentence, the "feel" of a sentence—even if they can't really remember the definition of a subject or of a verb. When students grok two-word sentences, it will be much easier for them to start groking sentences of all types. No, they won't stop writing sentence fragments overnight. They will, however, improve. The *feel* of a sentence will be with them. They won't have to think about definitions. They will grok the meaning.

When Tina Saw the Tortured Can Openers

Teaching dependent clauses does not have to be boring. In fact, the following activity actually allows students to have some fun with the subject. Give it a try.

1. Ask students to write five two-word sentences that they find interesting. Just for fun, you might even ask that the sentences also be alliterative, with both the subject and verb starting with the same letter. Examples:

    Sarah slipped. Greg groaned. Paul panicked. Molly moped. Carol collapsed.

2. Explain that each of the sentences they wrote is an independent clause. When a clause is independent, it can stand alone. (Of course, that means it is also a sentence.)

3. Explain that dependent clauses cannot stand alone. They must be part of another sentence. For example, this is a dependent clause:

    When Tina saw the Tortured Can Openers on HBO.

    Something is obviously missing. What happened when Tina saw the Tortured Can Openers? Here are just a few ways the sentence might be completed:

    When Tina saw the Tortured Can Openers on HBO, she fainted.

    *When Tina saw the Tortured Can Openers on HBO,
    she scowled and turned the channel.*

    *When Tina saw the Tortured Can Openers on HBO, she was more sorry than ever
    that her little brother had eaten her ticket to the concert in August.*

4. Show students that it is generally one little word that makes a clause dependent. *Tina saw the Tortured Can Openers on HBO* is a perfectly good sentence. Adding the word *when* makes it sound unfinished—and therefore a dependent clause. Here are some words that commonly introduce a dependent clause (also called a subordinate clause): *when, if, until, because, after, although, before, since, though, unless, until, whenever, while.*

5. Have students practice writing dependent clauses and attaching them to the five independent clauses they wrote in Step #1. Just for fun, ask them to make their dependent clauses as long, as detailed, and as interesting as possible. Examples:

Independent clause:
   Greg groaned.

Independent clause with a long dependent clause introducing it:
   After he looked in the refrigerator and found there wasn't anything at all to eat except for pickled herring and some moldy cottage cheese in an odd lime-green color, Greg groaned.

Independent clause:
   Paul panicked.

Independent clause with a long dependent clause introducing it:
   Because he saw something with at least eight long, furry legs crawling out of the top of his sock and starting up his leg, Paul panicked.

Independent clause:
   Molly moped.

Independent clause with a long dependent clause introducing it:
   When her parents told her she couldn't get a belly button ring and a nose stud for her grandparents' wedding anniversary party, Molly moped.

The Dorpersnoodle Assignment

Neatness Counts

C.M. Thurston

I'm not a persnickety old fogy. Honestly. Many people will scorn me for saying such a thing, but I believe it's true: Neatness counts.

Now I'm not talking about keeping a tidy notebook or a clean desk or even a spotless room. Many of us thrive in a somewhat chaotic environment with a lot of stimuli. How we manage our personal stuff is not the issue. What I am talking about is the importance of "presentation" in anything we give to another person for any kind of use or evaluation. Whether we like it or not, how things look is important. When we don't place enough emphasis on how things look, we are doing kids an ultimate disservice.

Here is one way to introduce the idea of careful presentation as you start out a new year with a new group of kids. Make your first assignment of the new year "The Dorpersnoodle Assignment." Silly as it may seem, it will get your students' attention. You will have set the stage, showing students that careful presentation is important in your class and *does* make a difference.

Of course, you may want to customize the "Dos" and "Don'ts" list on the student instruction page, to fit your specific requirements. However, it's a good idea not to overwhelm students with too many rules. It's also a good idea to have one or two "A" papers for students to look at as models—perhaps one that is typed, one that is written in ink.

The Dorpersnoodle Assignment

Neatness Counts

Here's your chance to start out the school year with an easy A. Your assignment is this: Turn in a one-page paper called "Dorpersnoodle." You can write an original story about a dorpersnoodle, or you can simply copy the following over and over again on the page: *Dorpersnoodles are fascinating. Dorpersnoodles are fascinating. Dorpersnoodles are fascinating.*

What's the point? The point is to practice presenting your work in a form that is neat and easy to read—without worrying, this time, about what you are saying. *What* you write will be important on every single thing you turn in for the rest of this year. This time, and this time only, *form* will matter more than content. The idea is to help you get in the habit of showing neatness and care in preparing all of your work.

For this assignment, concentrate on just one thing: making your paper look great. Pay attention to the guidelines below. Your class may even want to add some other "Dos" and "Don'ts" to this list before you get started.

DO:

- Use the heading your teacher prefers.
- Write neatly. If you really, really can't make your handwriting neat and legible, type your work.
- Give your paper a title. Capitalize it and center it.
- Skip a line after the title. Indent the first paragraph, and begin writing.
- Capitalize the first word of each sentence. Use a period or other appropriate mark at the end of each sentence.
- Use only one plain font for the body of the paper, if you are using a computer. (You can use a different font for the title, if you wish.) Don't use fancy fonts that are hard to read.

DON'T:

- Don't write to the edge of the page. Stop about an inch before the edge, at the red line that appears on most notebook paper.
- Don't write to the end of the page. Leave at least an inch at the bottom of the page, too. (Think picture frame: You are surrounding your writing with a white "frame.")
- Don't leave messy crossouts or scribbles on the page. If you are using pen and must correct something, just draw one line neatly through the mistake.

That's it! If you can turn in a paper that follows the guidelines above, you will have earned your first A for the year.

Hyperbole

A 6' 8" man unfolded himself from his little Porsche and started filling his gas tank. An elderly man standing nearby looked up at him and said, "Holy cow! Son, you're so tall you could hunt ducks with a rake!"

The tall man was a good sport and just laughed at the comment, even though it was rather rude. It was also an example of a technique often used in literature and poetry: hyperbole (hi-PURR-buh-lee). Hyperbole is a statement that exaggerates for emphasis or comic effect. It is not meant to be taken literally.

Here are some more examples of hyperbole:

- I could sleep for a year.
- This purse weighs a ton.
- I'm so hungry I could eat a horse.

- The trip took forever.
- There were a million people in line.
- He was as tall as a mountain.

Try your hand at writing sentences that include hyperbole. Be original. Don't use old sayings you have heard before. Write something new, choosing any 10 of the following 20 subjects. Use your own paper.

1. Describe how hot it is.
2. Describe how cold it is.
3. Describe how funny someone is.
4. Describe how boring something is.
5. Describe how handsome someone is.
6. Describe how thirsty someone is.
7. Describe how embarrassed someone is.
8. Describe how confusing something is.
9. Describe how happy someone is.
10. Describe how rich someone is.
11. Describe how big something is.
12. Describe how small something is.
13. Describe how angry someone is.
14. Describe how trendy someone is.
15. Describe how shy someone is.
16. Describe how loud something is.
17. Describe how messy something is.
18. Describe how sweet something is.
19. Describe how hyper someone is.
20. Describe how smart someone is.

Summarizing

Students are often asked to *summarize* something. Sometimes, unfortunately, they are a little confused about what that really means.

Summarizing simply means to sum up the main idea or main point of something, in far fewer words than the original. Whether or not you realize it, you summarize all the time.

Here's a real-life example. Suppose you have a little sister who comes home from school, upset, and tells you this story:

> *This girl in my class is, like, so mean! I hate her! When she came up to me today, I just knew she was going to say something terrible, and I was right! She stopped right in front of me and looked at my new coat and said, "Nice coat. Where do you shop, anyway? The Salvation Army?" Then she said I must be color blind to pick such an ugly color. No one paid any attention to her, but still, it made me so mad! It doesn't even make sense, either. I mean, her best friend has the exact same coat as I do and she doesn't make fun of her! Like, what is her problem? She always picks on me. I wish she would stop it!*

Your mother comes home, sees your sister stomping upstairs to her room, and says, "What's wrong with her?" Of course you don't repeat everything your sister said. You probably say something like this:

> *Samantha is upset because a mean girl at her school made fun of her new coat.*

You don't repeat everything she said. You don't give all the details. You hit just the essence, or main point, of what she said.

To summarize something you have read, you do the same thing. You cut through the details and look for the main idea or main point. Then you restate that point in your own words. Let's look at an example. First, here is a story about something in the news several years ago:

> *Luis Da Silva Jr. has become something of a star. You have never heard of him? You may have seen him, though. He is the bald, eighteen-year-old star of the enormously popular Nike commercial called "Freestyle 150." This two and a half minute music-video-style commercial has become all the rage, all over the country. According to ESPN.com, Da Silva dazzles "with his Harlem Globetrotter-like dribble moves...to the tune of the shoe-squeaking, hand-clapping, basketball-pounding, Stomp-reminding, hip-hop rhythm that has become the familiar background" of the commercial.*

Da Silva practices his moves in a small area of his backyard in Elizabeth, New Jersey. According to a story on the National Public Radio show "This American Life," Da Silva heard about auditions for the commercial at the last minute. When he showed up and started his amazing moves, those watching were in awe of his skills.

Now a summary:

An eighteen-year-old New Jersey boy named Luis Da Silva Jr. shows his amazing dribbling skills on the very popular Nike music-video-style commercial called "Freestyle150."

Now you try it. Summarize the following short article in one sentence:

Only a few short years ago, 20-year-old Kelly Clarkson from Burleson, Texas, was a cocktail waitress. Now she is a star. Clarkson sang her way to becoming the winner of Fox's "American Idol" television talent contest. Her new single, "A Moment Like This" was released on September 17, 2002.

In high school, Clarkson was a volleyball player and won important roles in high school musical theater productions. After she graduated in 2000, she had a number of jobs, including a job as a waitress in a comedy club and as a clerk at a pharmacy. However, she knew what she really wanted was a career in music. When Dallas auditions for "American Idol" were announced, a friend talked her into competing. Although there were around 1000 people auditioning in Dallas alone, Kelly kept getting callbacks. Finally, she was selected as one of 120 semi-finalists flown to Los Angeles for the American Idol competition. Week after week, she performed, and week after week, callers phoned in to vote for her. "Can that girl ever sing!" was the comment of many viewers during the competition.

In the end, Kelly Clarkson was proclaimed the "American Idol" winner and released her first single. Her song, "A Moment Like This," quickly became a hit. It made Billboard history by making the biggest single-week leap to number one in the history of Billboard's Hot 100.

Your one sentence summary:

Not all summaries have to be only one-sentence long, of course. Write a different summary of the Kelly Clarkson piece, but this time write a three-sentence summary:

Now, try your hand at summarizing a couple of paragraphs your teacher chooses from one of your textbooks. Remember: When you summarize, you use your own words to retell the main point or main idea. You don't include every detail. You select only the most important ones.

Activities
for Speech

Helping Students See that Speech Habits

DO Make a Difference

If your students are like most, they don't *say* things anymore. Instead, they *go* or they *like*. You probably hear conversations like this frequently:

> So Jason comes up to me and goes, "Will you be at the dance?" And I'm like, "Sure." And then he goes, "Good. Maybe I'll see you there," and I go, "Maybe," but really I'm like, "Omigod! I can't believe he said that!"

You also hear "likes" and "you knows" scattered meaninglessly throughout their sentences:

> I was, like, bummed out. Like, I couldn't, you know, believe she said that.

And that's just the beginning. Your students probably use dozens of other words and phrases that annoy you, and other people as well. Perhaps it's time for a speech lesson.

Speech is like clothing. Talk to your students about how we use speech, like clothing, to suit the occasion. For example, we might wear shorts and a tank top to a picnic but probably not to apply for a job. We might wear a jacket and tie to receive a special award from an organization, but not to run to the store for cat food.

Similarly, we often use different styles of speech for different occasions. If a person says "ain't" when talking to a friend at a party, the friend probably won't care. But if a person says "ain't" at a job interview, the employer may rank that person below another applicant who uses more "proper" English. Sometimes the employer may not even be aware of why he or she is doing so.

When people can change their speech to suit the occasion, there is no problem. The problem comes when they are unable to change, or when they are not even aware that their speech is sometimes inappropriate.

Seeing is believing. Fair or not, people form opinions of others based upon their speech habits, just as they form opinions based upon their style of dress. To help students see the impact speech habits can have on others, try the exercise "With Slang / Without Slang" (page 116).

The exercise includes two versions of a mock television interview, one with sloppy, "slangy" speech and one without. Choose some students to rehearse the interviews and perform them before the class.

(continued)

The students should be able to see that Author #1 and Author #2 have quite different effects upon an audience. Ask the students the following questions: Judging by what you have seen during the interviews, which person has more credibility? Which seems smarter? Which is a better writer? Which would you be more likely to take seriously?

Other ideas. There are many other classroom activities that can help students become aware of the importance of speech. Here are just a few ideas:

- Have students write two versions of a conversation between an employer and a person interviewing for a job. In one conversation, the person being interviewed should use poor grammar and a lot of slang. In the second, the person should use neither. Have volunteers read aloud some of the conversations, and let the class compare the impressions created.

- Help students learn to recognize "word puffiness." Word puffiness is the use of a lot of words to say very little. Most of the words are empty words and phrases, such as "you know," "like" and "well." Here's an example of word puffiness:

  She like, you know, wanted to go to the mall or, well, somewhere, you know, where there would be friends that she could like, you know, talk to.

- Have some volunteers (perhaps for extra credit) write out several examples of "puffy" conversations. They might want to make an audio recording of friends—with their permission—in order to come up with material. They might want to take notes while people are talking at lunch. Or they might want to jot down what people say in answer to questions during classes.

  Type the conversations. Then have the class reduce the conversations to clear, direct communication.

- At some point, students are likely to insist that they can stop using slang any time they want. See if that is true. Go on with class, but point out every example of slang used during discussion. If someone says, "We need more time to, like, study," ask, "Like study, or study?" Call attention to every *cheesy, lame, dude,* and *totally* used as slang. Have each student who uses slang start over, trying to eliminate the slang. Keep a sense of humor about this, of course. The point isn't to embarrass anyone.

  Chances are that conversation will come to a grinding halt. No one will be able to complete a sentence before someone points out that he or she is using slang. Students are likely to be surprised by how much slang they are using, and don't be surprised if you find out how much of it you use yourself.

- Pick out language pet peeves. Share your own and have students share any they might have, or any their parents or friends have. Examples: *these ones* instead of *these, babysitted* instead of *baby-sat, ain't got no* instead of *doesn't have any.* Many students may actually be unaware that there is anything substandard about words and phrases they frequently use.

    Be sure students understand that slang is an important part of our language and that there is nothing wrong with using it in the right circumstances. In fact, there are situations in which it wouldn't make sense to use anything but informal speech that includes slang. Have students think of those situations. (Examples: when trying to make friends at a new school, watching a football game, talking on the phone with your best friend, etc.) Then have students think of situations in which it would be wise to use more formal language. (Examples: giving a speech, interviewing for a job, taking phone messages at work, meeting your mother's boss, etc.)

- Talk about the importance of choice—the ability to choose what kind of language to use, according to the circumstances. When a person hasn't learned anything but sloppy speech patterns, that person doesn't have a choice. He or she must talk the same way in all circumstances, and that can have unfortunate consequences. Have the students brainstorm some of those consequences. (Examples: creating a bad impression with a date's parents, having some people think you are less intelligent than you really are, being unable to get certain jobs, like radio announcer, television reporter or public information officer.)

With Slang/Without Slang

Conversation #1

TALK SHOW HOST: I'd like to introduce our next guest, Lila Harrington, who is here to tell us about her new book, *American Schools Today*. Welcome, Ms. Harrington.

AUTHOR #1:   Dude! What's up? Glad to be here!

TALK SHOW HOST: Can you tell us why you wrote your book, Ms. Harrington?

AUTHOR #1:   Sure. Well, see, like, it was a couple a years ago and I was, like, teaching in a school, a middle school. I was, you know, really gettin' into it—teaching, I mean. Then, see, one day I read this article about all the bad stuff going on in schools—you know, like drugs and violence and kids not learning nothing and stuff like that. And I'm totally like, "That's not *my* school." So I go, "You know, maybe I oughta write a book." So, like, I did!

TALK SHOW HOST: I see. And what is your book about, exactly?

AUTHOR #1:   Well, it's about, like, good stuff, you know, good stuff going on in schools. It gives you a real good picture of kids today.

TALK SHOW HOST: And how do your students feel about the book?

AUTHOR #1:   They're like, "Wow! Ms. Harrington! That's, like, awesome!" They're really, like, soooooo blown away that I'd do something like that.

TALK SHOW HOST: I'm afraid we have to go now, Ms. Harrington. Thank you for speaking with us today.

AUTHOR #1:   Thanks a lot. Later!

Conversation #2

TALK SHOW HOST: I'd like to introduce our next guest, Lila Harrington, who is here to tell us about her new book, *American Schools Today*. Welcome, Ms. Harrington.

AUTHOR #2: Thank you.

TALK SHOW HOST: Can you tell us why you wrote your book, Ms. Harrington?

AUTHOR #2: Yes. Two or three years ago, I was teaching at a junior high and really enjoying it. Then one day I read a newspaper article about all the negative things happening in schools today—drugs, violence and so little learning taking place. I found myself thinking, "That's not *my* school!" I knew a lot of very positive things were going on in my school and in schools where my friends taught. So I came up with the idea of writing a book myself.

TALK SHOW HOST: I see. And what is your book about, exactly?

AUTHOR #2: It's about all the positive things that are happening in schools today. I wanted to show the world a more optimistic view of education.

TALK SHOW HOST: How do your students feel about the book?

AUTHOR #2: They think it's wonderful. They are so impressed that one of their own teachers would write a book—a book about them.

TALK SHOW HOST: I'm afraid we have to go now, Ms. Harrington. Thank you for speaking with us today.

AUTHOR #2: Thank you for inviting me.

Helping Students See the Power
of Being Positive

Just before students are to give speeches or class presentations, try the following experiment. It can help class members see that attitude and behavior can affect others, and that students can help one another by being part of a positive audience.

An experiment in positive reinforcement. Ask for a student volunteer, explaining that you need someone to be a guinea pig in a class experiment—someone who isn't afraid to talk, someone who is willing to get up in front of the class and speak. Choose a volunteer who is a good sport, and then ask him or her to step out of the room and take a few minutes to prepare a speech on the subject of "school" (or another topic you approve).

In the meantime, explain to the rest of the group that the students are going to be a part of the speech. How? The students will participate through their reactions. The left half of the room is to react positively, giving only positive reinforcement to the speaker, no matter what he or she says. Explain that these students are to look at the speaker, smile, nod, look fascinated, etc.

The students on the right half of the room, however, are to give only negative reinforcement. They are to look away from the speaker, doodle, pass notes, look bored, stare out the window, yawn, whisper to one another, etc.

Have each side practice their parts for a moment. (You may need to suggest that the negative side of the room not overdo it.) Then explain that you want the students to observe what happens to the volunteer when he or she speaks.

When the volunteer returns, have him or her stand exactly in the front of the room, at a podium if possible. Look at your watch and tell the volunteer to begin speaking.

In a very short time, you will see that the volunteer begins talking to the "positive" side of the room. He or she will look at that side of the room more and will soon start ignoring the negative side. He or she will probably turn physically toward the positive side, perhaps even moving over to that side of the room. In some class experiments, the speakers have actually picked up the podium and moved it to the positive side of the room!

After three minutes or so, depending upon how well the speaker holds up, stop the speech and explain what the class has been doing. Ask the volunteer how he or she felt. Ask the class members what they observed. Discuss with the group how people respond well to positive reinforcement. You may also ask the students to think of ways they could use positive reinforcement in their own lives—for example, in teaching a brother or sister something, helping someone with homework in a difficult subject or working with team members at athletic events.

Lessons in Grammar & Punctuation

Grammar Ideas for Teachers

Who Hate Teaching Grammar

C.M. Thurston

Check any of the following items that describe you:

❑ You hate the way your students' eyes glaze over at the mere mention of adjectives and adverbs.

❑ You think there are more important things to do in class than have students underline subjects once and predicates twice.

❑ You wonder why you're supposed to teach gerunds and participles to kids who haven't yet mastered starting a sentence with a capital letter.

If you checked two or more of the items, the ideas below are just for you. They are dedicated to all the English teachers in America who secretly—or not so secretly—hate teaching grammar.

• Try bribery. No, this doesn't mean passing out chocolate chip cookies for correct answers. It means getting your students to agree to this offer: less time on grammar in exchange for their complete attention and effort.

  When you start a unit on, say, adjectives, explain that there are two ways to handle the unit: (1) The class can study adjectives for weeks and weeks. During that time the students can stare into space, yawn, write notes, surreptitiously do their algebra and endlessly repeat phrases like, "I hate this stuff!" and "Why do we have to do this, anyway?" Or (2) The students can agree to concentrate, learn what they are supposed to learn, and be done with adjectives as quickly as possible. Agree that you will spend only a short amount of time on grammar—if the students cooperate— and then go on to something more interesting.

  It is helpful to set a goal with the students—for example, to cover Chapter Two in the book and pass a test by Friday.

• Do mini-units all year long, rather than long sessions on grammar. For example, spend a day or two on prepositions; then go on to something else. In a month, do another day or two on prepositions. Repetition in small doses helps avoid burnout—and helps students remember better, as well.

• Keep a sense of perspective. You can spend weeks studying objective and nominative cases, hoping to get students to understand how to use *who* and *whom* correctly. But why take so much time? Many believe the distinction between the two words is fast disappearing. It may be better to just touch upon the topic, especially for the benefit of your skilled writers, and then spend more time on something more important.

- Don't confuse grammar with mechanics. Students should know how to punctuate and capitalize correctly. However, they don't need to know much grammar in order to do so. For example, suppose you want students to learn that they should use a comma with a coordinating conjunction in a compound sentence. You can spend time teaching them coordinating conjunctions, more time teaching them compound sentences, and even more time teaching them the rule. Or you can take a different approach that is likely to be more effective.

  Show the students a list of compound sentences, all punctuated correctly. Have them try to figure out what the sentences have in common. Help them come up with a guideline—in words they can understand—for punctuating similar sentences. (For example, they might come up with something like this: Sometimes writers connect two whole sentences with the words *and*, *but*, *or*, *for*, or *nor*. When they do that, they need a comma right before the connecting word.) Have the students make up similar sentences of their own, punctuating them correctly.

  Another effective method of teaching mechanics is to use examples of incorrect sentences from student papers. Jot down incorrect sentences as you grade papers. Then, once a week or so, put four or five of the sentences on the overhead, without names. Go over the sentences with the students, helping them to see the mistakes. Then give them some new sentences with the same errors and have them try to correct these sentences on their own. Repeat this lesson frequently throughout the year, and you will cover just about everything your students are ready to learn about mechanics and punctuation.

- Don't take the grammar book too seriously. If yours is like most, you can poke fun at a number of things. For example, the sentences in the exercises are often excruciatingly dull, dated, or even rather bizarre. Don't be afraid to laugh at them. I once found myself shaking my head at some sentences about frozen vegetables in a grammar book. I wondered why on earth the textbook authors thought such a subject would be interesting to ninth graders. I said as much to my students and, surprisingly, found them paying more attention after that. It became a game to find and point out sentences just as boring as the frozen vegetable sentences. The game helped many students keep from completely tuning out.

  Another thing you can laugh at is the way the explanations and rules are often written. It sometimes seems as if the book is trying to make things as difficult as possible. Challenge your students to rewrite material so that it makes sense to young people. For younger students, try introducing an imaginary character like Seymour Fendlehessy, the worst English student in the world. Have the students rewrite a lesson in the book so that even Seymour can understand it. To do that, of course, the students will be forced to pay close attention, sorting out the material first for themselves.

- Students are bound to complain about all the exceptions to the rules. Try telling them this: "This rule or guideline won't work all of the time, but it will work about 95% of the time, which isn't bad. And by the way, 95% is an A."

  Or, if you are brave, have them try to look for exceptions to the rules. It will help them pay attention.

- Trust your instincts. If something seems impossible for your students' skill level, it probably is. Don't try to do the impossible.

- Don't get bogged down in rules. Students aren't likely to remember rules. Instead, they need a "feel" for doing things correctly.

  For example, I once tutored remedial writing students on a college campus and had a student whose writing was simply terrible—a hodgepodge of sentence fragments that made little sense. The boy couldn't understand what was wrong, and yet he knew this rule well: *A complete sentence has both a subject and a verb.* The problem was that he found subjects and verbs everywhere. He thought every noun he saw was a subject. He saw gerunds and thought they were verbs. He found verbs in subordinate clauses and thought the clauses were complete sentences. He knew the definition of a sentence, but he had no sense or *feel* for a sentence.

  I had to unteach the boy, insisting that he forget the definition he knew so well. Instead, I had him read aloud lists of sentences, then lists of fragments. Almost immediately, he heard the difference. He couldn't explain the difference, but he heard it. After more practice in just hearing the difference, he was able to distinguish between complete sentences and fragments. Soon he eliminated the problem he had been having with sentence fragments, and his writing quickly improved.

- Try not to feel frustrated that your students have so much trouble with grammar. Students have trouble learning something before they are ready for it, and perhaps elementary, middle school and junior high students today just aren't ready for grammar. Let's face it; today's video game generation has little experience with the written word. Often our students are struggling with the very basics of writing while we are trying to teach them to identify participial phrases and subordinate clauses.

  Perhaps the study of grammar needs to be limited to older students who have already mastered the basics of composition. Children learning to talk don't have to analyze what they are doing. Perhaps children learning to write need the same freedom.

Prepositions Are Boring Words

Prepositions are boring words. *Of, on, after, into* and *with* are all prepositions, and they are not very interesting. Interesting words are words like *giggle, millionaire, crunch, Mars, pizza, howl, wow, gigantic* or *puppy.* Interesting words are never prepositions.

Although prepositions are boring words, they are also very important words. They are everywhere. Look at this list of frequently used prepositions:

> about • above • across • after • against • along • among
> around • at • before • behind • below • beneath • beside
> between • beyond • by • during • for • from
> in • inside • into • like • near • of • off • on
> over • out • through • to • toward • under • until
> upon • with • within • without

These are words that we see, read, hear and say a lot. They aren't very exciting words, but they certainly are useful. We use prepositions primarily to show relationships between words. What does that mean? It means that a preposition can show where something is in relation to something else.

For example, imagine a desk. Now imagine a book. Where could that book be in relation to the desk? It could be *on* the desk, *in* the desk, *beneath* the desk, *near* the desk, *above* the desk, *beside* the desk, *below* the desk, etc. *On, in, beneath, near, above, beside* and *below* are prepositions showing where the book can be in relation to the desk. Another way to think of it is like this: A preposition often shows the position of something.

Important hint: One of the most commonly used prepositions is *of,* which just doesn't fit the description of a preposition very well at all. You just need to remember that *of* is one of the most common (and most boring!) prepositions of all.

Practice with prepositions.

1. Use all of the prepositions in the list above in sentences. However, see how few sentences you can use. Can you use them all in just seven sentences? Five sentences?

_____

_____

_____

2. See if you can write five sentences about a person—but without using any prepositions. Make each sentence at least seven words long.

_____

_____

_____

_____

_____

Prepositional phrases. A preposition usually needs to be completed. It isn't enough to say *beyond* or *near* or *without* or *through*. Beyond what? Near what? Without what? Through what?

Prepositions need to be completed because they usually occur in prepositional phrases. It's not enough to say the keys are *in*. In what? If they are *in the car*, you have a prepositional phrase. A prepositional phrase begins with a preposition and ends with a something, i.e., a noun. The phrase includes all the words in between that preposition and the noun.

For example, we might say, "The keys are in the new car," or "The keys are in the shiny new car." *In the new car* and *in the shiny new car* are both prepositional phrases. If we say, "The keys are in the car with the sun roof," we have two prepositional phrases. Can you tell what they are?

Here are some more examples of prepositional phrases:

over the rainbow	*in my shoes*	*of the United States*
with the principal	*after the dance*	*inside a cardboard box*

Prepositional phrases often occur in "strings," one right after the other. Can you pick out the prepositional phrases in the following string?

I pledge allegiance to the flag of the United States of America and to the Republic . . .

More practice with prepositions. Find the prepositional phrases in the sentences that follow. (Not all sentences have them.) Remember—a prepositional phrase begins with a preposition and ends with a noun. Put each prepositional phrase in parentheses, like this: I pledge allegiance (to the flag) (of the United States) (of America) and (to the Republic) . . .

1. Joshua sat at a desk at the back of a math classroom.

2. He ignored his teacher and stared at the girl in the next row, who was sitting beside a window and doodling in her notebook.

(continued)

3. The girl had a rose tattoo, brown hair with a barrette in it, and a nice smile.

   (Hint: *A, an* and *the* are boring words, but they are not prepositions. They don't show a relationship. *And* is not a preposition either. Check your work so far. Have you marked any of these words as prepositions? If so, correct your work.)

4. Suddenly the girl turned and smiled at Joshua.

5. Joshua smiled back and winked.

6. The teacher said, "Joshua, why don't you stop flirting and concentrate on page 21?"

7. Joshua scowled and looked back at his book.

8. The girl smiled, turned the page of her notebook and started writing a note to Joshua.

9. That night Joshua's math book sat at home by itself on the floor of his closet.

10. At the local Pizza Hut, Joshua sat beside a girl with a rose tattoo. They were eating a giant pizza with pepperoni and mushrooms.

Activities with Adjectives

Did you know that nearly everything you say or write is filled with adjectives? Adjectives are everywhere, adding interesting spice, color and flavor to our language. If you write a note to a friend about a funny movie you saw, you are using an adjective. If you complain about a *boring* class, you are using an adjective. If you ask for *chocolate* milk at lunch, you are using an adjective.

So what are adjectives? Adjectives are describing words. They describe nouns. They give more information about nouns. Where do you find adjectives? An adjective most commonly appears before the noun it describes. Look at the examples below.

    fluffy kitten   *fluffy, gray* kitten   *a fluffy, gray* kitten

(Note: A, *an* and *the* are always adjectives. Sometimes they are also called articles or article adjectives. When you see *a, an* or *the*, you know that a noun is coming up.)

A. If a word is an adjective, it will usually sound right if you say it before the noun you think it describes.

Examples:
   Yes: *lively* puppy   *sleepy* puppy
              frisky puppy   *Joshua's* puppy

   No: *trouble* puppy

(Although a puppy may be a lot of trouble, *trouble* isn't an adjective because, all alone, it doesn't describe the puppy. It also doesn't sound right to say "trouble puppy.")

Think of four adjectives to describe the halls of your school.
_____ halls   _____ halls   _____ halls   _____ halls

Think of four adjectives to describe a car.
_____ car   _____ car   _____ car   _____ car

(continued)

B. See if you can find the adjectives in the following sentences. Underline each adjective and draw an arrow to the noun it describes.

1. A green dragon climbed into the dark castle and kidnapped the beautiful, sleeping princess.

2. A giant, fuzzy spider was crawling in Chad's hair.

3. The tall, handsome boy wearing a brown leather jacket walked into the math classroom and smiled at Denise.

C. Underline all the adjectives in the following paragraph. (Hint: There are 21, counting the article adjectives and the possessive pronouns used as adjectives.)

Michael and his date sat down near the back of the movie theater. He smiled at her as they shared a giant-sized box of buttered popcorn and two small Cokes. The overhead lights faded, and they turned their attention to the wide screen. Then Michael heard a familiar voice. "Hi!" whispered his little sister and her best friend, slipping into the seats right behind him. Michael groaned and muttered, "Why me?"

D. Write a paragraph about a musical group or a television show that you like. However, see if you can use *no* adjectives, except for *a, an* and *the.*

E. Sometimes an adjective occurs *after* the noun it describes.

Examples:

Mary is *brave.*
Joe looks *puzzled.*
I am *tall.*

Write five sentences with adjectives occurring after the nouns they describe. (Hint: If you have trouble, try using some of these verbs in your sentences: *is, am, are, was, were, looks, feels, tastes, seems.*)

F. Cut out an article from a newspaper. Underline ten adjectives in the article.

G. See if you can write one sentence with ten adjectives in it.

H. Write a menu for a party, using at least ten adjectives.

Examples:

tomato soup

French bread

I. Make a poster. Look through magazine and newspaper advertisements and cut out ten sentences with adjectives that describe various products. Arrange the sentences on your poster, along with pictures of the products, and underline all the adjectives.

Using Quotation Marks

An Introduction

This is Linda.

This is David.

This is a cat.

Linda likes cats and David does not.

Now let's put all this information together into a cartoon.

It's easy to see what each character above has said. The "balloons" coming out of their mouths contain their words.

Now let's take David and Linda out of the cartoon and put them in the middle of a story:

"Oh, what a beautiful cat!" said Linda. "I love cats. They are so smart and independent."

"Ugh!" David frowned. "Get it away from me. I hate cats. They are so unfriendly and stubborn."

"Meow," said the cat.

We no longer have balloons to indicate who said what. Instead we have quotation marks to help us. The quotation marks are used in much the same way as the balloons. They enclose a speaker's words, and to do that they must always come in pairs.

Of course Linda didn't say the words *said Linda*. That's why these words are not enclosed by quotation marks. She did say, "Oh, what a beautiful cat!" That's why those words begin and end with quotation marks. Quotation marks are used only around the words that a character actually speaks.

Notice that quotation marks are not used around every sentence. One set of quotation marks goes at the beginning of a character's words; another set isn't needed until the words are interrupted with material like *he said*—or when the character is finished speaking.

Notice also that the paragraph changes each time the speaker changes. The first paragraph is indented because Linda is speaking. A new paragraph begins when David begins speaking. Another begins when the cat "speaks." New paragraphs make it easier for the reader to follow the conversation, especially if it is a long one.

Direct and indirect quotations.
When you use a character's exact words, you are using a direct quotation. Sometimes, however, we tell what people say without using their exact words. Then we are using an indirect quotation. Let's look at an example.

> *Linda saw a cat and said that she thought it was beautiful. She loves cats. David,*
> *who hates cats, told Linda to get the cat away from him. He thinks cats are*
> *unfriendly and stubborn. The cat just meowed, expressing no opinion on the subject.*

Here we know the ideas Linda and David are expressing, but we don't know their exact words. These indirect quotations do not need quotation marks. Here's another example.

Indirect:	*He told her he loved her.*
Direct:	*"I love you," he said.*

Look at the items below and decide which ones are direct quotations and which ones are indirect quotations. Put an "I" beside each indirect quotation. Put a "D" beside each direct quotation and add the quotation marks needed. Remember, quotation marks always come in pairs.

1. _____ Jim's mother said she would ground him for a month if he didn't clean his room right away.

2. _____ Jim's mother said I will ground you for a month if you don't clean up this pig-pen of a room. Today!

3. _____ My sister always wants anchovies on her pizza said Kristen. The rest of us gag at the smell of them.

(continued)

4. _____ I hate boys who are conceited remarked Melanie. I also hate it when they show off all the time.

5. _____ Julie said she was going to go out for basketball, but her father said she would have to bring up her grades first.

6. _____ Greg was at the mall Friday night when he saw a girl he liked. He asked her to go get some frozen yogurt with him, and she said she would.

7. _____ Michael didn't have much confidence. I'm going to flunk. I'm going to flunk. I'm going to flunk, he repeated over and over to himself as he took the math test.

8. Write an indirect quotation about a movie. Make the speaker a girl named Kaylie.

_____

_____

_____

_____

9. Write a direct quotation about a movie. Make the speaker a boy named Scott.

_____

_____

_____

_____

10. Write a short conversation between Scott and Kaylie, having them discuss a movie.

_____

_____

_____

_____

_____

_____

_____

_____

The Apostrophe

What is an apostrophe?

"Apostrophe" is a big word, but it is a name for something very small. It is the name for a kind of punctuation mark. Let's take a look at an apostrophe:

,

That's it. An apostrophe is just one little mark. But perhaps you are thinking, "It looks just like a comma."

So it does, at least as it appears above. That's because it's just hanging there, in the middle of nowhere. If it were in a line of print or handwriting, it would be easy to see the difference. A comma is written at the bottom of a line of print or writing. An apostrophe, on the other hand, occurs above the line of print. Look at the examples that follow:

Comma: *Bill lived in Portland, Oregon.*
Apostrophes: *Bill's mother didn't live in Portland.*

What do you do with an apostrophe? Apostrophes are very important marks of punctuation.
Best of all, they are easy to learn. Here we are not going to learn about every possible, unusual, once-in-a-lifetime use for the apostrophe. Instead, we are going to learn the basics about this little mark. If you learn these basics, you will know all you need to know about apostrophes for about 95% of the writing you will ever need to do.

There are two main uses for the apostrophe. Apostrophes have two main uses. They are
used for (1) contractions and (2) possessives. Contractions and possessives are long names for some simple ideas. Let's look at these words one at a time, starting with contractions.

What are contractions? Contractions occur when we contract two words into one. For example,
most of us wouldn't say, "We are going to walk downtown." Instead, we would say, "We're going to walk downtown." We contract *we* and *are* into a new word, *we're*. The apostrophe indicates that we left something out, in this case the letter *a*.

That is the first use for an apostrophe.

In a contraction, an apostrophe is used to indicate that letters are left out.
The apostrophe takes the place of the missing letters.

(continued)

Here are some more examples of contractions: *he's, doesn't, aren't.* Write four more contractions in the spaces below:

1. _____ 2. _____ 3. _____ 4. _____

What are possessives? When something is ours, we possess it. To possess means simply to own or to have. When we write, we often use an apostrophe to indicate possession. For example, let's say that a girl named Katie has a cat. When referring to that cat, we might say, "Katie's cat." See that apostrophe? You might think of it as "hooking" Katie to what she owns. The apostrophe and the "s" connect Katie and her cat, indicating ownership.

Here are some more examples of an apostrophe and an "s" indicating that someone has or owns something:

> *the police officer's badge*   *Bob's stereo*
> *my mother's secretary*   *the teacher's grade book*

Sometimes it is not a person who owns or has something. For example, you might write about *the factory's cooling system.* The apostrophe and "s" indicate that the cooling system belongs to the factory. Or you might write about *the book's title page* or *the painting's frame* or *the truck's headlights.*

Sometimes the "thing" that is owned or possessed is not something you can see. Sometimes it is a quality or an idea. For example, we might write about *John's love for Mary* or *Carolyn's idea for the skit* or *Mark's goal for the game.*

Let's review the second use for an apostrophe.

An apostrophe is used to indicate possession.

Practice writing possessives. Rewrite each of the phrases below so that you use an apostrophe with an "s" to show possession.

Example: the car that belongs to John
_____ John's car _____

1. the new dress that belongs to Tammy

_____

2. the anger Mary has toward Bill

_____

3. the capital of the nation

_____

4. the puppy that belongs to the child

_____

Plural nouns. So far, we have been talking about singular nouns—in other words, one person or thing owning something. What happens when you talk about plural nouns? In other words, what happens when more than one person or thing owns something?

The answer is, "It depends." Sometimes you add an apostrophe and an _s_. Sometimes you add just an apostrophe. There's a very easy way to tell which to do.

First, ask yourself, "Who owns or has this?" Then look at the answer. If the word does not end in _s_, add an apostrophe and an _s_. If the word does end in _s_, simply add an apostrophe.

For example, suppose we want to write about clothing for men in a department store, and we don't know whether to write mens' clothing or men's clothing. First we would ask, "Who owns or has this clothing?" The answer would be _the men_. _Men_ does not end in _s_, so we would add an apostrophe and an _s_, like this:

men's clothing

But suppose we wanted to write about a bicycle that belonged, jointly, to two boys. We would ask, "Who owns or has this bike?" The answer would be _the boys_. Because _boys_ already ends in an _s_, we just add an apostrophe, like this:

the boys' bicycle

Don't make this more difficult than it needs to be. In other words, don't do anything but add an apostrophe or an apostrophe and an s. For example, if you want to write about the trophies that belong to a family, you would write the family's trophies. You would not do anything else, like change the _y_ to _i_ and add _es_. Again, all you do is add an apostrophe, or an apostrophe and an _s_.

(continued)

More practice writing possessives. Rewrite each of the phrases below so that you use an apostrophe with an *s*, or just an apostrophe to show possession.

> **Example:** books that are for children
> *children's books*

1. a Christmas party for the family

   _____

2. a large crib shared by two babies

   _____

3. a Christmas party for three families

   _____

4. a locker shared by two students

   _____

5. the department for women

   _____

The apostrophe disease. Beware! There is danger in studying apostrophes. After they study apostrophes, many students catch the apostrophe disease. In other words, they start throwing apostrophes everywhere, whenever they see the letter *s*. They write about having two sister's and two sweater's and a bunch of pencil's. One student even wound up writing the word *is* as *i's*.

Please be careful not to catch this disease. Apostrophes do not belong everywhere. They belong only in contractions and in words that indicate possession. If you are in doubt about possession, ask who owns what. Examples: *Joanie's car.* (Does Joanie own the car? Yes. *Joanie's* is a possessive.) *The chairs' in the room?* (Do the chairs own the room? No. The phrase should read simply *the chairs in the room*—with no apostrophe.)

Teaching Sentence Structure

Without Teaching a Lot of Rules

Students can learn a great deal about sentence structure without learning a lot of definitions and rules. The following lesson is designed to do several things:

- to help students see that sentences have patterns
- to help students recognize some basic sentence patterns, but without using grammatical terminology
- to give students practice in writing complete sentences
- to help students see how commas fit into some basic sentence patterns

Procedure

1. Put the following sentences on the board or on an overhead transparency:

    - Meredith ate a hot fudge sundae.

    - Meredith ate a hot fudge sundae with nuts and whipped cream.

    - Meredith ate a hot fudge sundae with nuts and whipped cream and a cherry on top.

2. Explain that sentences can be like rivers—they flow. Often they flow without bumping into anything. The three sentences above are like that; they flow without bumping into anything. For purposes of this lesson, we will call sentences that flow, with no interruptions, *main sentences.*

3. Explain that sometimes "stuff" interrupts the flow of a main sentence. That "stuff" can come anywhere in the sentence—at the beginning, in the middle, or at the end. The "stuff" is separated from the main sentence with a comma or commas. Show your students the following examples:

    - *Interruption at the beginning of the sentence:*
      Knowing that she would ruin her dinner, **Meredith ate a hot fudge sundae.**

    - *Interruption in the middle:*
      Meredith, knowing she would ruin her dinner, **ate a hot fudge sundae.**

(continued)

- *Interruption at the end:*
  Meredith ate a hot fudge sundae, knowing she would ruin her dinner.

Prepositional phrases at the end of a sentence are considered part of the main sentence. However, if a prepositional phrase occurs out of its natural order and introduces a sentence, then it is considered introductory "stuff." Show your students the following examples:

- *Main sentence:*
  James left for school with a can of Pepsi in his jacket pocket.

- *Interruption at the beginning:*
  With a can of Pepsi in his jacket pocket, **James left for school.**

4. Have the students find the main sentence in each example below:

   - Racing down the hall as fast as he could, Jeremy tried to make it to his first period class on time. (Main sentence: Jeremy tried to make it to his first period class on time.)

   - Robert went to the movie early, hoping to get a seat near the front. (Main sentence: Robert went to the movie early.)

   - Stacie's little sister, who was a tattle-tale, ran outside before Stacie could strangle her. (Main sentence: Stacie's little sister ran outside before Stacie could strangle her.)

5. Have the students complete Part A of "Sentence Structure" (page 139). After going over Part A, introduce students to sentences that contain two main sentences (compound sentences). Then have the students complete Parts B and C.

Note: The concept of "main sentences" is useful only in helping students see patterns in sentence structure. Don't analyze it too much or ask for perfection. Most students will catch on quickly and, as a result, have a better understanding of how sentences are constructed.

Sentence Structure

Part A

Underline the main sentence in each sentence below. (Remember: If a sentence has no "stuff" interrupting it, the whole thing is the main sentence.)

1. The students at Washington Junior High, which is located on the south side of town, scored well on the district physical education test.

2. Using her parents' car for the first time since she got her license, Tammy drove her friends to the dance.

3. Smiling at the class, the speaker began his talk with a joke.

4. The first grader eagerly walked to school with his mother.

5. The storm raged across the city, causing the superintendent to cancel school.

6. A dead frog lay on the table in biology class, waiting to be dissected.

7. Jason worked hard to improve his grade in science.

8. When Maria opened the door to her closet, dozens of boxes crashed to the floor.

9. My best friend Linda, seeing that the best-looking boy in the school was standing beside the water fountain, decided that she was dying of thirst.

10. Overwhelmed by all the new faces, the new student walked into the classroom, trying not to look as nervous as he felt.

Check your work from Part A before you go on to Part B.

(continued)

Part B

Sometimes two main sentences can occur together in the same sentence, held apart by one of these words: *and, but, or, for, nor* (and sometimes *yet* or *so*). As you underline the main sentences below, see if you can find the sentence with two main parts.

1. Cruz dropped his books all over the floor.

2. Angela's favorite teacher, Mr. Garcia, was just elected teacher of the year.

3. Steve sat quietly at his desk, his eyelids drooping.

4. When Melanie walked into the kitchen, her mother sat at the table, the newspaper spread out in front of her.

5. To tell you the truth, most teachers don't particularly like to grade papers.

6. Most students, on the other hand, secretly enjoy homework.

7. Jo Ann went to the game, and there she bought a huge tub of popcorn.

Part C

Now write some sentences of your own, following the instructions below.

1. Write a sentence with interrupting "stuff" at the beginning.

2. Write a sentence with interrupting "stuff" in the middle.

3. Write a sentence with interrupting "stuff" at the end.

4. Write a sentence with two main sentences in it.

The Semicolon

The following lesson is both a lesson in thinking and a lesson in how to use semicolons. Students themselves examine material and, with teacher guidance, form and test a generalization about the primary use for the semicolon. Then they practice using what they have learned.

1. Make a transparency or photocopy of "Impress Someone; Use a Semicolon" (page 143). With the class, read aloud the introductory material. Then ask the students to look carefully at the sentences in Section A as they read them aloud, looking for what they think the sentences have in common.

2. List their answers, trying not to judge whether or not their observations are correct. (Kinds of responses students might make: All end in periods. All have subjects and verbs. On each side of the semicolon, there is a complete sentence. Each side is about the same length. All the sentences could have periods where the semicolons are. Each half of each sentence is about the same subject as the other half. None of the sentences have little words like *and*, *but*, *or*, *for* or *nor* connecting them.)

3. Ask the students whether or not they think any of the observations listed are incorrect. Eliminate any that the class, as a whole, thinks should be eliminated.

4. Next, give this instruction: Using the information from the list you have just made, take a few minutes and see if you can make up a general rule to explain how to use a semicolon.

   Have the students work individually for several minutes on this task; then have them share their results. (Kinds of responses students might make: Use a semicolon when you think two sentences kind of go together, but a comma isn't enough. Use a semicolon when you want to connect two closely related, complete sentences that each stand alone. Use a semicolon when there is no *and*, *but*, *or*, *for*, or *nor* connecting two sentences that are on sort of the same topic. Use a semicolon when you could use a period, but the sentences seem to go together.)

5. Choose (or let the students choose) one rule to work with. Ask if there are any modifications the students would like to make to the rule before they test it. Write the finished rule on an overhead transparency.

(continued)

---

6. Have the students look at the sentences in Section B, which show semicolons used incorrectly. Give this instruction: All the sentences in Section B show semicolons used incorrectly. If the rule you just made up is correct, each of these sentences should violate that rule in some way. Do they? If so, how? Do you want to make any modifications to your rule?

7. Have the students do one last check. The sentences in Section C show sentences with semicolons used correctly. Ask the students to check to see if their rule holds up with these sentences. By this time, the students should have arrived at a rule something like this: A semicolon can be used between two complete sentences that are closely related in subject matter. The part to the left of the semicolon should be able to stand alone; the part to the right of the semicolon should be able to stand alone as well. (You may need to point out that the semicolon actually takes the place of a period or a connecting word like *and, but, or, for* or *nor*. Students should also have noticed that a capital letter is not used after the semicolon, unless, of course, the following word is a proper noun.)

8. When everyone (including you!) is satisfied that the rule holds up, pass out student copies of "Practice with Semicolons" (page 144). Have the students copy the rule in the space provided. Then have them complete the worksheet, using their new rule as a guideline.

Impress Someone; Use a Semicolon

Semicolons are impressive; not many people know how to use them correctly. However, there is a little-known secret about the semicolon: it is an easy punctuation mark to learn to use. It can be used in several ways, but it has one primary use—which you will soon discover for yourselves.

Here is what a semicolon looks like:

;

(like a comma with a period above it.)

Section A (semicolons used correctly)

1. John wanted to rent the DVD *Pirates of the Caribbean*; Jenny wanted to rent *The Sisterhood of the Traveling Pants*.
2. Today I'm going to make my plans; tomorrow I'm going to act.
3. Jeremy adored his little sister Shelly; in fact, he spoiled her rotten.
4. Sam puzzled over the decision for days; he simply couldn't make up his mind.
5. Nicole was hoping Michael would ask her to the dance; however, she agreed to go with David when he asked her.

Section B (semicolons used incorrectly)

Wrong: 1. There are several ways to ask someone for a date; a phone call, a written invitation, a simple question, begging.

Wrong: 2. I never want to see you again; and I wish you would go jump in a lake.

Wrong: 3. He raced to the finish line; sweat pouring down his face.

Wrong: 4. I hate apricots; I'm going to get a new coat for my birthday.

Section C (semicolons used correctly)

1. He begged his father to buy him a new car; however, his father refused.
2. Cream the butter and brown sugar; add the milk to the mixture and beat well.
3. She wants to be president of the United States when she grows up; she also wants to be a quarterback and a princess.
4. Mr. Cabella loves to watch "Dancing with the Stars" on Monday nights; on Sunday nights he loves to watch "Desperate Housewives."

Practice with Semicolons

Semicolon rule or guideline decided upon by the class:

_____

_____

_____

_____

Using the rule above, put semicolons wherever appropriate in the sentences below. (Note: some sentences may not need semicolons at all.)

1. Elizabeth loved Scott Scott loved Karen.

2. John wanted fish, but Casey wanted hamburgers.

3. Emily knew she should be studying for her history test however, she really wanted to pull the covers over her head and go to sleep.

4. I never saw a purple cow I never hope to see one.

5. Marie likes to do the dishes right after dinner her husband Michael likes to put them off until morning.

6. Marie thinks Michael should have to scrub the dried food off the dishes when he insists on leaving them until morning, but he thinks they should just buy new dishes.

7. Teachers are wise students are not.

8. Students should not become upset about sentences like #7.

Now write three sentences of your own, correctly using semicolons. Make the sentences about anyone or anything mentioned in items 1-8, above.

_____

_____

_____

_____

Thank Heaven for Pronouns

Be grateful for pronouns. Imagine how boring and repetitive our language would be if we didn't have those noun stand-ins like *you, he, she, they, me, your, his, hers, theirs,* etc. Here's how things might sound:

> Jack was walking with Jack's cafeteria tray when Jack saw Raina sitting at a table with an empty chair beside Raina. Jack smiled at Raina, and Raina smiled back. Jack asked if Jack could sit down with Raina. Raina smiled shyly and said, "Sure."
>
> Jack and Raina ate quietly for a moment, and then Jack said, "Would Raina like some of Jack's Tater Tots?"
>
> Raina said, "Yes." Then Raina said, "Raina's friends are having a pizza party for Raina's birthday on Friday. Does Jack want to join Raina and Raina's friends?"
>
> Jack said, "Sure. Jack thinks going to Raina's party sounds great."
>
> Patrick was sitting beside Jack and Raina. Patrick couldn't stand it anymore. "Please use pronouns!" Patrick yelled. "Stop sounding like idiots!"

Rewrite the paragraph above so that it includes pronouns. Underline each pronoun that you use.

Then add a paragraph that tells what happened after Patrick yelled. Use at least 10 pronouns in your continuation of the story.

Activities for Different Seasons

This Year, I Hope

As you begin a new school year with your students, ask them to think about their hopes, dreams and goals for the next year. Explain that you are going to ask them to write something to be turned in and used later but that no one else will see without their permission. Then ask each student to complete the following sentence, in at least ten different ways:

This year, I hope...

After students have listed at least ten of their hopes, ask them to study their lists. Which hopes are impossible hopes? Which hopes might come true? Which hopes depend completely upon the actions of others and are thus out of the students' control? Which hopes could their action, or lack of action, possibly help to come true?

Ask students to write a paragraph or two about their hope lists. What do they think their lists tell about themselves, about their lives, about the world around them?

Have students fold their papers in half and staple them shut, placing their names on the outside. (Or bring envelopes and have the students put their letters inside, addressing the envelopes to themselves.) Explain that you will save the papers to be given back to the students during the last month of school.

At the end of the year, pass back the lists and have students reread them. Ask them which of their hopes came true and which ones did not. Ask them how much effect their own actions had upon whether or not their hopes were realized. Have the students discuss and/or write about their reactions to reading what they wrote nine months earlier.

Name_____

September Brain Strain

Can you earn at least 200 points by following the instructions below?

1. Write the word SEPTEMBER across the top of your paper, followed by the same word
    written backwards. You should have this written on your page:

    S E P T E M B E R R E B M E T P E S

2. Now write a sentence (or several sentences) with words that begin with the letters above, in
    order. (The first word in the first sentence must begin with *s*, the second word with *e*, the
    third with *p*, etc.) Try to use all the letters in as few sentences as possible.

    Scoring: If you are able to use all the letters in one sentence, give yourself 75 points.

    If you are able to use them all in two sentences, give yourself 60 points.

    If you are able to use them all in three sentences, give yourself 50 points.

    If you are able to use them all in four sentences, give yourself 40 points.

    If you are able to use them all in five or more sentences, give yourself 30 points.

    Score (subtotal): _____

3. There are six *e*'s across the top of your page. Write a sentence that uses at least six words
    that begin with *e*.

    Scoring: If all the words in your sentence begin with *e*, give yourself 60 points.

    If only one word begins with a letter other than *e*, give yourself 50 points.

    If two or more words begin with letters other than *e*, give yourself 40 points.

    Score (subtotal): _____

4. Write one sentence or more with words beginning with only the consonants across the top
    of your page, in order.

    Scoring: Follow the same scoring as in Item #2.

    Score (subtotal): _____

5. Repeat any of the steps above, using entirely different sentences, to earn more points.

TOTAL SCORE: _____

Fears

Fears are a natural subject in October. Halloween, after all, has traditionally included many frightening subjects, such as ghosts, witches, goblins, and monsters.

Take a moment to think about fears. Then answer the questions below.

1. What are you, or people you know, afraid of? List some common fears in the space below. (Examples: spiders, heights, hospitals)

2. You probably listed fears that were on the lists of many others in your class. Now think a bit harder. What other fears are shared by many people your age? You might include silly fears, embarrassing fears, or very serious fears. (Examples: your mother coming to school wearing something weird, having someone break into your house, losing someone you love)

3. Now think about a time you were very afraid. (Examples: hearing noises late at night after watching a horror movie, being in a car accident) Try to recall details of the time you were very afraid. Jot down some details that describe how you felt at that time.

4. Can you think of any examples of things people perhaps ought to be more afraid of? (Examples: drunk driving, air pollution) Why should they be more afraid than they are?

(continued)

5. Do dreams ever frighten you? What scares you the most? Do you ever have the same dream more than once? What details do you remember about an especially frightening dream?

6. Do your thoughts ever frighten you? Think of a thought that has frightened you, perhaps because it seemed evil, unkind, or upsetting in some other way. You may jot down the thought below, or you may want to keep it to yourself. If you keep it to yourself, see if you can describe *why* the thought was so frightening.

7. What other thoughts do you have about the subject of fear? Jot down any ideas that come to mind, and consider sharing your ideas with the rest of the class.

Writing about fear. Choose a writing topic based on the general topic of fear. Look over your notes on these two pages, and think about what was discussed in class. Then choose one specific topic for your paper. Here are just a few ideas, but you will probably be able to think of many more:

- What Fears Have in Common
- The Secret Fears of Teenagers
- How Fears Are Different at Different Ages
- The Most Frightening Few Moments of My Life
- My Most Frightening Dream
- What Scares Me Most About My Life
- What Scares Me Most About the World
- How Fear Can Be Useful

Not for the Squeamish

In October, newspaper ads and feature stories tend to take on a spooky quality, featuring goblins, ghouls, ghosts, and other subjects not for the squeamish.

Squeamish. Say the word aloud. Listen to it.

Squeamish. It's got an interesting sound. So do other words in our language that begin with "sq."

Your challenge. Put the 20 *sq* words below into an October newspaper-style story. Your story must make sense, though it will probably have to be a bit farfetched in order to include all the words.

Newspaper stories answer the questions *Who? What? Where? When? Why?* and *How?* They often include a quotation of some kind by someone involved in the story or by an official commenting on something about the story.

Remember also that newspapers have limited space. See how short you can make your story and still have it make sense. Good luck!

1. squabble
2. squad
3. squalid
4. squall
5. squander
6. square
7. squash
8. squeak
9. squeal
10. squeamish
11. squeegee
12. squeeze
13. squelch
14. squid
15. squiggle
16. squint
17. squirm
18. squirrel
19. squirt
20. squish

No More Gore

You are a screenwriter specializing in horror films. However, the company that produces your movies has been receiving a lot of criticism lately about the amount of violence in its films. Bowing to public pressure, the company has just adopted a new policy: *No more gore.*

That means your new assignment is going to be a real challenge. The company wants you to write a script that (1) will be scary, (2) can be rated "G" and (3) has absolutely no "blood and guts" scenes in it. You know you can write a movie to fit these requirements, even though you are used to writing about chain saw massacres and hatchet murders. You will just have to proceed slowly, step by step:

- First, think about what makes a movie frightening. For example, people often shriek in the theater when something or someone jumps out unexpectedly. What else scares people? Brainstorm a list of things that can frighten a movie audience.

- Next, imagine what your movie is going to be about. Who will be the main characters? Where and when will it take place? How will horror enter the story?

- Finally, write the opening scene, a scene that will get the audience interested—and frightened—right away. Describe what happens, including dialogue for any characters that speak. Follow a format something like the one you used for your previous movie, *Killer Pigeon:*

> *The movie opens with a little girl and a little boy chasing butterflies in a meadow. The girl is about five years old, with long, black hair. She is wearing a pink, ruffled dress. The little boy is about the same age. He is wearing a suit and tie, but there is chocolate smeared on his face. We know it is late afternoon, for the sun is low in the sky, just about to go behind the mountains in the distance. The background music is the sweet sound of violins, coming from a wedding reception visible in the distance.*

> LITTLE BOY: *I'm going to catch one before you.*
> LITTLE GIRL: *No, you're not! I'm going to be first!*

> *The little girl reaches up to grab a butterfly in her hand. Suddenly, there is a tremendous roar, something like the roar of a lion, only more mechanical sounding. The little girl freezes, staring into the distance. She doesn't move. She doesn't even blink her eyes. The little boy, on the other hand...*

- For a real challenge, perhaps as extra credit or a special class project, finish your movie script. Make the script appropriate for a short film, ten to twenty minutes long.

I'm Thankful for Weekends,

My Kitten, My Baby Brother's Giggle...

Part I. Many people today believe that American society has become too materialistic. Grade school children insist on the "right" brand of jeans or sneakers. Teenagers work long hours at part-time jobs to pay for cars or to buy trendy clothes. Adults go into debt to pay for expensive cars, homes, furniture, hot tubs, computers, vacations, etc. Some people believe Americans today value *things* more than ideas, knowledge or even people.

Do you agree or disagree that Americans today are too materialistic? Do you think that young people are more or less materialistic than adults? Discuss your ideas with the class, and listen to what others have to say. Then write a paragraph or two giving your views on the subject.

Part II. Thanksgiving is traditionally a time when people take a look at all they have to be thankful about in their lives. Often they tend to look at the big things—their families, their homes, their health, etc.

For a change of pace, make a list of the little things in your life that you are thankful for—nonmaterial things only. In other words, don't list a new basketball or a new cell phone. Do list items like these:

• the way my best friend always saves a seat for me on the bus

• my mom's hug when I tell her about a problem

• the way Mr. Cornwall never makes me feel dumb in math for asking a question

• my friend Jamal's jokes

• the way the second lunch lady in the cafeteria line always smiles and never gets grouchy like the others

Thanksgiving "T" Time

For a Thanksgiving challenge, try this game. Announce a category. Then have students, in small groups, list as many words as possible that begin with the letter *t* and fit the category. For example, if the category is *animals*, groups might list *tiger* and *tarantula*.

It is important to keep the game moving. As soon as you see students slowing down with a category, change it. One to three minutes per category usually works well. Groups score one point for each correct answer.

Below are some categories to try:

1. Boys/girls names
2. Adjectives used to describe a roller coaster ride
3. Things people are afraid of
4. Foods that make your stomach turn
5. Adjectives used to describe basketball player LeBron James
6. Five-letter words
7. Names of sitcoms
8. What you do on Saturday
9. Verbs
10. Words that end in *e*
11. Adjectives your grandmother might use to describe styles she doesn't like
12. What you do in physical education
13. What you might bring if you go camping
14. Things used in sewing
15. Adjectives used to describe a cowboy
16. "Nice" words to describe your teacher
17. Words that end in *ly*
18. Synonyms for junk
19. What you do on an average school day
20. Baseball terms
21. Modes of transportation
22. Things that are annoying
23. Games (indoor and outdoor)
24. Things you can do at a dance
25. Beverages
26. Sounds
27. Words that begin with *trans*
28. Things you can do in the city
29. Things you can do in the country
30. Adjectives to describe the Empire State Building
31. Things you don't like about school
32. Things you do like about school

Curing December Doldrums

It's hard to get students to concentrate on anything during December. Their thoughts are often on the holidays, vacation, parties—anything but school. Composition work, like all work, can be difficult at this time of the year.

Try making things easy on the kids—and on yourself—by using all that holiday excitement as a springboard for writing. For a week, have the students write for ten minutes or so each day on a different holiday topic, choosing from the ideas listed below and adding ideas of your own. (It's a good idea to offer a choice of topics each day.)

Explain that the audience for the daily writing assignments is ultimately going to be the rest of the class. Take time to let the students talk about each topic before they begin writing.

After five days of writing, have the students meet in groups of four to read each other's work. Each small group determines which piece in each person's collection is the most interesting to share with the class.

Next, each group decides how it wants to present its four chosen pieces to the class. Different individuals might read aloud the chosen papers—not necessarily their own. (Students who die of embarrassment reading their own papers sometimes enjoy reading aloud someone else's.) A group might bring in an outside person, like the principal, to read a paper. Another might choose to type papers, photocopy them and pass them out to the class. Some students might want to record their papers, perhaps with appropriate sound effects or even videotape someone reading each paper. Encourage the students to be creative in deciding how to present their work.

Don't feel that you must grade all the papers; December is a busy time of the month for you, too. Instead, enjoy the sharing that will occur in the class and, with luck, the real efforts to communicate. If you must give a grade, try giving each group a grade on the effectiveness of its final presentation (which, of course, will have included the students' written work).

Writing topics

1. How did you find out the truth about Santa Claus? Explain. How did you feel? What did you do? What did you say? How did others around you react?

2. Describe the best gift you ever gave. What made it special? How did the person who received it react?

3. Describe the worst, funniest or most unusual gift you have ever received.

4. Think of someone close to you. Now describe the perfect gift for this person, the gift you would give if anything were possible.

(continued)

5. Describe the worst holiday you remember. What happened? What made it so bad?
6. Describe the best holiday you remember. What happened? What made it special?
7. If you could change anything about this time of year, what would it be? Why?
8. What funny holiday stories are told in your family? Tell your favorite.
9. Describe your holiday plans—the plans you *wish* you had.
10. Describe holiday traditions in your family. Do you share traditional foods? Are there traditions you follow, according to your family's heritage? What about religious ceremonies, rituals, meals, games, gifts, etc.?

Always Wear Clean Underwear

Mothers always have advice for their children. They tell them to wear clean underwear, in case they are in an accident. They tell them not to speak with their mouths full. In answer to "Everyone else is doing it," they say, "If everyone else were jumping off a cliff, would you jump, too?"

In honor of Mother's Day, ask your students to think about some of the words of advice they have received from their mothers or from a mother figure in their lives. Brainstorm with the class to make a list of things mothers always seem to say. This part of the activity can be fun; don't be afraid to laugh at the similarities that are bound to occur. Students may even wonder if mothers everywhere have a book to consult, perhaps a book called *What to Say if You Are a Mother.*

Then ask students to think more seriously about advice their mothers give them. Ask them, for the next week, to write down pieces of advice their mothers give them. Have them spend some time trying to remember good advice from their mothers. Ask them to think of times they followed their mother's advice and it paid off—or times when they didn't and wished they had.

At the end of the week, have everyone write a paragraph or two on "My Mother's Advice." You might then put together a handout called "Advice from Our Mothers," for students to take home for Mother's Day. You could include the advice the students brainstormed as a group, as well as selections from the individual paragraphs.

Variation. After students finish writing about advice from their mothers, ask them to try the same idea, focusing instead on advice from fathers. Then have them compare the two sets of advice, discussing the differences between what their mothers tell them and what their fathers tell them.

Another idea is to have students interview their mothers, asking them to tell about the advice they got from their mothers when they were young. Have them discuss how advice from the different generations is the same, and how it is different.

Sports Mania

National Physical Fitness and Sports Month—May

In honor of National Physical Fitness and Sports Month, see how quickly and accurately you can complete the items below.

1. List 20 different sports.

2. List 20 well-known athletes, 10 female and 10 male.

3. List 20 common terms used in sports. List the term and then the sport it is used in. (Example: *batting clean up: baseball*)

4. List 20 different well-known team names. (Example: *Denver Broncos*)

5. List 20 places where sports are commonly played. You may list general places like "a baseball field" or specific places like "Yankee Stadium."

6. List 20 things a person might have to do in a physical education class.

7. Make up a sports category of your own and list 20 items that fit the category.

75 Ideas for the Last Month of School

1. Have the students write about how they have changed this year. What have they learned about themselves? Others? How have they grown? What goals have they met? If students kept journals or daybooks throughout the year, they might look through them for ideas. You might also ask students to consider how their writing itself has changed.

2. Plan a word game day. It might even be a reward for meeting specific classroom goals. "English" on page 177 is one suggestion for an absorbing game students will enjoy.

3. Plan an award day. Make certificates and give each student an award of some kind, whether serious or just-for-fun. Examples: best job of chewing gum without getting caught, most creative compositions, most improvement, funniest class comments, best excuse for not turning in work.

4. Have students practice descriptive writing. Spend fifteen or twenty minutes outside, having everyone just sit, observe and write about what they see, hear, feel, taste, smell. Students will enjoy both the fresh air and a legitimate excuse to be out-of-doors.

5. Plan a trip to Bermuda for the day after school is out. Think about Bermuda whenever things get tough.

6. Have each student rank this school year on a scale of 1-10 and tell why he or she chose that ranking.

7. Play "Hangman" or "Pictionary" or "Trivial Pursuit" when you have extra minutes before class ends.

8. Have a no-talking day where everyone—including you—communicates with writing, sign language (informal or formal), pantomimes, etc.

9. Take snapshots of your class and put them up on a bulletin board. Use them as prizes for end-of-the-year activities, but save one to add to a gallery display of all your past classes.

10. Have students bring in baby pictures for a display. Then have them write an early childhood memory. After several days of guessing who is who, post the compositions beside their authors' pictures.

11. Give someone a break. Let a student turn in something late. Give someone the extra three points needed to earn an "A." Accept a flimsy excuse. Hope (or even ask) that your kindness will be passed on to someone else.

12. Remember to smile more.

13. Have students write letters to themselves, to be mailed back in five years. Have each provide a self-addressed, stamped envelope. One Colorado teacher does this every year, and students are delighted five years later to read their own thoughts about themselves.

(continued)

14. Spend some time on oral communication. Pick an ordinary paragraph from a magazine. Then have students take turns reading the paragraph, altering the wording if desired, and pretending to address different audiences: a church congregation, an audience at a rock concert, a teachers' meeting, etc.

15. Start an end-of-the-year journal to record your thoughts—positive and negative—about the previous nine months. Be sure to record your successes, no matter how small, and also include what you would like to do better on next year. Once you get into the habit of summarizing each year, you will be delighted to look back at your teaching record and see how you have changed, how you have improved.

16. Take a field trip. Take a lot of field trips.

17. Pretend that it's January and do nothing at all out-of-the-ordinary. (Perhaps the students won't notice it's almost summer?)

18. Start each day with review questions from all year. Make a game or challenge of it.

19. Secretly do something nice for someone else in your school each day. It might be an anonymous gift, a note of appreciation, a small favor. Giving something positive to someone else will help you feel more positive yourself.

20. Spend any remaining English department money on a belly dancer to entertain the kids.

21. Just kidding.

22. If you're feeling brave, try "story time" with your junior high or even high school students; it can be great fun. Simply have the students take turns reading aloud children's books, thus giving individuals a chance to "perform" and the class a chance to be entertained. (You might even serve milk and cookies!) Follow up by having the students write their own children's books or stories.

23. Have students write about the two or three things they remember most about class this year.

24. Play popular music and have students pick out poetic devices—alliteration, rhyme, metaphor, simile, etc. The students will be reviewing terms from your poetry unit and enjoying songs at the same time. (Let the students bring in the music, but screen the songs by insisting on seeing a written version of any song before you play it. Otherwise you might be in for some shocking surprises.)

25. Play a dictionary game. Each student uses the dictionary to find five nouns he or she doesn't know. Then the student writes a multiple choice question about each noun, hoping to stump the class later. Sample question: Is a *mastiff* (a) a sail on a ship, (b) a dead butterfly, (c) a large dog, (d) a religious ceremony?

26. Get plenty of exercise. It will help your attitude.

27. Consider "forgetting" a set of papers if you get behind (which you will). It isn't necessary to grade absolutely everything you assign.

28. Get in the habit of saving one of your favorite units until May each year. Your enthusiasm will help keep students interested in class.

29. Have the students write about "Little Things that Would Have Made this Class Better this Year" and "Little Things I Appreciated in Class this Year."

30. Pat yourself on the back more. Practice saying, "Good for me, I graded all those papers." or "Good for me, I didn't lose my temper when Kelly asked me the same questions I'd just spent ten minutes answering."

31. Videotape some commercials and do a unit on propaganda techniques. See if students can learn to recognize the propaganda techniques they see in commercials.

32. Take a crash course in stress management.

33. Treat the teacher's lounge to fresh-ground coffee.

34. Invest in a portable fan. If your classroom is miserably hot, it may be worth it. You can even resort to bribery then, telling the kids that you will leave the fan on only as long as they are calm and on task.

35. Dress up a little. If you start appearing more and more casual as the weather gets warmer, you may be sending the kids a signal that things are really over for the year.

36. Avoid strangling anyone. It does not look good on your resume.

37. Make a game out of end-of-year drudgery like check-out sheets. (If you can think of a way to do this, please share. We all need to know.)

38. Take time for Warm Fuzzies Day. Give each student slips of paper, one for every person in class including yourself. Spend a quiet period in which each student writes at least one positive thing—anonymously—about each person in class. Collect and screen the slips; then pass them out the next day. The students will love them.

39. Pick a great book and spend a few minutes each day reading aloud. Don't be afraid to read aloud just because your students are out of elementary school. Junior high and high school students can surprise you.

40. Have the students write trivia questions about their school. Allow questions about teachers, the building, classes, or any person likely to be known by most students. Use the questions as "fillers" for odd moments, or compile them for a "School Information Scavenger Hunt" for your class. You might even save the scavenger hunt questions to use with new students next fall, to help orient them to your school.

41. Stop berating yourself for the stack of papers you haven't managed to file all year. Stop worrying that you will have to file them all neatly before you go home for the summer. Instead, put them into boxes to be filed next fall, when you are fresher. Perhaps by then you will even have the courage to close your eyes, grit your teeth and throw them all away.

(continued)

42. Have each student write a "letter from my desk" to the unknown person who will sit in the desk next year. Have the students give advice, describe what to look forward to, tell about what to expect, etc. Then use the letters with your new students next fall.

43. Have some restless students clean out your middle desk drawer, boxing loose paper clips, dusting, tossing leaky pens. (Do a quick check first, though. No student needs to examine the plastic bag containing an extra pair of panty hose or the overdrawn notice from your bank.)

44. If you can, avoid doing anything "final" before the last day of school. For example, a final test given three days before school is out can set the wrong tone for the last three days.

45. When your class seems rowdy and out of control, think about the teachers whose classes are worse than yours. It won't make your kids behave any better, but it will make you feel better.

46. Offer to give your principal some hands-on experience back in the classroom. Surely he or she would *love* to teach a class or two for a change, especially during the last week of school?

47. Try a discussion day. Have students sit in a circle and take turns completing sentences: "The best thing about school is..." "I'm afraid of..." One thing that worries me is..." Let students elaborate and discuss the comments after each round.

48. Lighten up. Remember that kids are kids. Too often we expect them to act mature, forgetting that they aren't supposed to be mature. They are kids.

49. Blank out the words in several cartoon strips and photocopy the cartoons. Have students write their own dialogue for the cartoons. Then have them transfer the dialogue to paper for practice in writing and punctuating conversation.

50. Introduce a unit on gerunds, infinitives and participles for the last week of school.

51. Do the above only if you are absolutely out of your mind.

52. Have a poetry memorization contest. With a selection of classics for students to choose from, see which team of students can memorize the most poems. (Weight the poems, giving more points for longer ones, fewer points for shorter ones.)

53. Write a silly letter to the class, mentioning as many student names as possible. (If you do this frequently, you won't have to get *all* their names in every time.) Fill it with errors of all types—spelling, capitalization, punctuation, run-ons, fragments, etc. Divide the class into small groups and see if any group can manage to correct everything in the letter.

54. If you keep a file of book reports students have made during the year, spend a period or two having the students make notecard-sized book covers to represent each book. Then post all the covers on a bulletin board, letting students see how much they have accomplished over the year. (The covers will need to be small so that you have enough room.)

55. Give a lot of lectures about how school isn't over yet and the kids had better shape up and improve their attitudes. (It won't do any good, and you know that, but you will do it anyway. Because the kids hear the same thing all day long from all their teachers, perhaps you could pick a student to give the lecture for you now and then, just for variety.)

56. Don't work on weekends.

57. If you manage the above, please take a bow.

58. Try to avoid having school-aged children of your own to come home to at night. Dealing with kids at home and at work is asking a lot of anyone.

59. Play "Newspaper Scavenger Hunt" in *Surviving Last Period on Fridays and Other Desperate Situations* (Cottonwood Press, Inc.) for three days. It keeps the kids absorbed and interested, and it gives them practice in skim reading, following directions and working together as a team.

60. Set up a fake incident. For example, have the principal come in and yell at you. Argue, get upset, and perhaps knock over a vase of flowers, spilling water everywhere. After the incident, ask the students to write about what they observed. Read aloud several different versions of what happened (They are likely to be very different). Talk about how our powers of observation are often less than accurate in emotionally charged situations.

61. Have speakers with "real life" jobs come in and talk about why reading and writing is so important in their work.

62. Design a "Pat on the Back" form for students to fill out for anyone who deserves a thank you. Give some suggestions to get the students thinking: the school secretary who gave you a hug when you came in furious because everything had been stolen from your locker, your math teacher for cheerfully giving you extra help at lunch every day until you finally understood division of fractions, your friend who let you use her biology notes to study for a big test after you lost your own notes. Allow the forms to be anonymous or signed. Screen them, fold and staple them, and let a team of volunteers deliver them.

63. Talk a lot about the way things were when you were in school and how easy the kids have it nowadays. (Students love that. It gives them something to groan and roll their eyes about.)

64. Try this homework assignment: Talk to an adult about one important thing he/she learned in school. Why was it important? When did he/she learn it? From whom? Where? How has it been useful? Get as many details as possible and then write a paragraph about what you learned in your interview.

65. Start class with silent reading for the last few weeks of school. The activity is worthwhile and has the added bonus of calming the kids down. For added encouragement, you might make your last grade of the year a book report.

(continued)

66. Have your students spend a period in the library with this assignment: *Each of you is to discover three truly interesting facts, pieces of trivia, or ideas to share with the class tomorrow. Record the source for each. You and the other students are responsible for class tomorrow. If the items you choose are boring, everyone will be bored. If the items you choose are interesting, the class should be an interesting one.*

67. Start class each day with a brain teaser or a puzzle, just for fun.

68. Hug a lot.

69. End class each day with two or three minutes of "improv." Google "improv theater activities" for a wealth of ideas.

70. Have the class practice their writing and speaking skills by producing and videotaping a school news program, "This Year at Our School."

71. Make a class "Memory Book" for the year.

72. Write notes to parents of students you really enjoyed in class this year—but not necessarily just good students. Did someone's sensitivity towards others impress you? Say so. How about someone who was especially responsible, someone who stood up for what was right? Parents and students both love specific notes of praise and are likely to cherish them for years.

73. If you feel absolutely frustrated, depressed, stressed-out, or close to tears—try humming. Do it under your breath, in the car, in the restroom. It's hard not to cheer up just a bit when you hum, no matter how badly you do it. Make a game of it with other teachers. Hum or sing to each other. Don't be afraid to be a bit silly now and then.

74. Consider paying someone to help you out this time of year. Could a high school or college student grade some papers or enter data into your computer, for just a few dollars an hour? Could you afford to hire someone to clean house for you, just until school is out? Think creatively about ways to lighten your load at a very busy and stressful time of year. The cost may be well worth it.

75. Be proud of yourself! You are doing one of the most important jobs in the world: teaching young people.

Spring 100 Challenge

The goal of the "Spring 100 Challenge" is to earn 100 points by writing sentences with words that begin with the letters in *SPRING*, in order. Here's how to score points:

10 points. Score ten points for each six-word sentence. The first word must begin with S, the second word with P, the third word with R, the fourth word with I, the fifth word with N, and the sixth word with G.

> Example: *Someone predicted rain in northern Georgia.*

- All sentences must make sense, even if they are a little strange.
- Each sentence must be substantially different from the other sentences you write. ("Substantially different" means that no more than two words can be the same. In other words, if you receive 10 points for a sentence that begins "Sarah paid...," you cannot receive another 10 points for a sentence that is exactly the same except that it begins, "Spencer paid...")

Less than 10 points. If you write a sentence that begins with the letters of *SPRING*, in order, but you need to add some other words in between to have it make sense, subtract one point per word added. For example, if you add 2 extra words, your score will be 10 minus 2, or 8 points.

> Example: *Six politicians (were) re-elected into (the) new government.* (8 points)

5 points. You may also write six-word sentences that begin with the letters in *SPRING*, but in any order. For example, the first word in the sentence might begin with G, followed by words beginning with P, N, R, S, and I. (The same rules about making sense and being substantially different apply.) Each sentence is worth 5 points. You may add extra words without subtracting a point.

> Example: *Gum never is right (to use in) public school.* (5 points)

How many points can you score?

Hint: It helps to make a list of all the verbs you can think of for each letter. Each sentence has to have a verb, and verbs are harder to think of than nouns.

Games

"Verbing" Down the Alphabet

Write a story that uses verbs that begin with all the letters of the alphabet, in order. After a verb that begins with *a*, use a verb that begins with *b*, then a verb that begins with *c*, etc. (There can be other verbs in between. In other words, your story can have many more than 26 verbs.)

For example, you might start a story like this:

> Sabina <u>a</u>dored cats and <u>b</u>rought her darling Puffmellow with her everywhere. One day, she was <u>c</u>ruising down the highway in her Honda when she saw a sign that said, "Cats for Sale." She had always <u>d</u>reamed of having another cat, so she immediately pulled over. "I think you may soon have a sister. It will be wonderful!" she <u>e</u>xclaimed to Puffmellow. Puffmellow <u>f</u>rowned and <u>g</u>ave her a look that said, "Put that idea out of your head immediately..."

Longer and Longer

A Letter at a Time

See how long a sentence you can write, having each successive word one letter longer than the last.

Start with three letters. The first word should have three letters. The second should have four letters. The third should have five letters, and so on. Score one point for each letter you use.

Example

The tall hiker yelled angrily. (25 points)

Then try the same thing, but beginning with one letter, then two letters, etc.

Challenge. Try to earn 100 points by writing more than one sentence following the guidelines above.

Vocabulary Puzzle

Use a dictionary or www.dictionary.com to answer the questions below.

1. Which of the following doesn't belong? Why?

    yew, yohimbe, yagi, yarrow

2. List 25 words that begin with *t* and can be used as nouns.

3. Put the following words in alphabetical order:

    industrious, indented, gentle, immaculate, ink, intestine, inevitable, incredible, insight, cow, improbable

4. Which one of these would you definitely *not* find in a musical group?

    theorbo, bodhran, ocarina, ocelot

5. Which one of these might be considered unsafe?

    pannier, parapet, paraquat, patagium

6. Rewrite the following sentence so that it is easier to understand:

    When the curmudgeon encountered the beneficent crone,
    he experienced transient tachycardia and became enamored.

7. Which of the following would best describe a good speaker? Why?

    verbose, obtuse, articulate, sesquipedalian

8. List the 12 signs of the zodiac in alphabetical order.

9. Define *adze*, and then name three professions that would be likely to use one.

10. Use *rabbit* and *rabbet* correctly in one sentence.

11. Which of the following words has one syllable? Two syllables? Three syllables? Four syllables?

    emulate, mollusk, flapjack, salamander, grommet, squelch, pendulum, emu, goblin,
    spatula, oblong, haddock, knoll, smidgen, flipper, peppercorn

12. Would you rather be a *spelunker* or a *numismatist*? Tell what each does, and then explain your choice.

13. Which word doesn't belong in the following list? Why not?

    algid, hiemal, sweltering, gelid, brumal, rimy, niveous

14. Name ten things that are *xanthic*.

15. Which two of the following words should you never use in writing or speech? Why?

    exigency, exorbitant, expedite, exasperate, excape, exuberant, excerpt, exculpate, expecially, excoriate

Whining

"I hate it when..."

Tyler and Brooke like to complain. Wherever they go, they whine about little things. People have started to groan whenever they see Tyler and Brooke. They are tired of listening to all their complaints.

One day their teacher decided that Tyler and Brooke needed help. She said, "I want you to make a list of all the little things in the world that bother you—all of them. Get the whining out of your system."

Tyler and Brooke came up with a long list. However, they did not proofread their list. See if you can locate and correct the 50 spelling errors in Tyler and Brooke's list. Don't guess. Be sure your corrections are correct.

1. I hate it when the pizza crust is soggie. I also hate it when the hot cheeze burns the roof of you're mouth.

2. I hate it when you think your opning a plastik contaner of leftover tuna and it turns out to be a contaner of something green with purpel fuzzy mold growing on it.

3. I hate it when the seatbelt in the car hits me in the neck becuz I'm to short.

4. I hate it when I can't find the remoat control.

5. I hate it when my sister is watching something stoopid and won't give me the remoat control.

6. I hate it when my mom puts tofoo in things and hopes I wont notice.

7. I hate it when the peperoni on the pizza isn't evenly devided and I get a slice with only won peice of peperoni on it.

8. I hate it when it's time too go and my mom cant find her keys.

9. I hate it when my cat upchucks a hairball on my bed.

10. I hate it when someone finishs the milk and puts the empty cartun back in the refrigerater.

11. I hate it when my parents try too act cool around my freinds.

12. I hate it when I get a pimple rite between my eyebrouws.

13. I hate it when I get a pimple any where.

14. I hate it when someone steps on the back of my shoe and makes it come of.

15. I hate it when my parents are on a diet and we have to eat baked fish.

16. I hate it when my parents turn off my stereo and say, "Aaaaah . . . . silunce!"

17. I hate how my friend eats her Reese's Peanut Butter Cups by nibling the choclate completely off before she gets to the peanut buter part.

18. I hate it when my dad asks quesions like, "Who is this Tommy Hilfiger?"

19. I hate it when my sister gets on the phone and it kiks me off the Internet.

20. I hate how my sister chews off all of her fingernales instead of cuting them like a normal person.

21. I hate it when the mashed potatos touch the peas on my plait.

22. I hate it when my shoelases get cought in my bicicle spokes.

23. I hate it when my mom makes me bring my little brother along when my friends and I go to the maul.

24. I hate it when I'm trying to read and the nieghbor's dog wo'nt stop barcking.

25. I hate it when my teacher makes me right a list of all the things I hate.

Now add 10 items you hate to the list. Be sure to proofread your work, of course.

_____

_____

_____

_____

_____

_____

_____

_____

_____

_____

_____

_____

_____

_____

_____

_____

_____

Lipograms

A lipogram is a sentence or paragraph that does not include a certain letter of the alphabet. Create a lipogram by rewriting the following sentence to eliminate the letter *t*:

> *Robert took his time reading the cartoon pages in the Saturday morning paper*
> *while he ate his toast and drank his tea.*

Possible answer:

> *On a morning following Friday, Bob slowly read comics from a newspaper*
> *while he consumed his crispy-surfaced bread*
> *and drank his cup of H2O flavored by a small herb-filled bag.*

Create a lipogram by rewriting the following sentences, eliminating the letter indicated.

1. Eliminate the letter c. *After snoozing on the cushy carpet and consuming some catnip, my crazy cat likes to chase mice.*

2. Eliminate the letter f. *Billy often has fun frolicking with his frisky puppy and throwing a frisbee for him to fetch.*

3. Eliminate the letter s. *Julie doesn't like to study on Saturday or Sunday night because she's tired after attending college classes all week.*

4. Eliminate the letter w. *Sam wanted to take a walk around the lake, but the wind was blowing too hard.*

Now create some lipogram puzzles of your own to share with the class. Be sure to include a possible solution to each puzzle.

English

For each category on the left, think of an appropriate word that begins with the letter at the top of the column.

	E	N	G	L	I	S	H						
Boys' names	Eric												
Five-letter words													
Animals													
Sports													
Proper nouns													
Things with wheels													
Fruits													
Girls' names													
Words that end in *e*													
Countries of the world													
Words that might be used as verbs (action words)													
Cartoon characters													
Movie titles													
Last names of nationally-known athletes													

Did You Really Fall Into a Vat of Anchovies?

Using Little-Known Facts for Classroom Exploration   C.M. Thurston

A student once told me that, as a child, she had fallen into a vat of anchovies in San Francisco. So I told her about the dimple I have, made by a screen door hook that caught in my open mouth and poked itself all the way through my cheek. Then I told her about my childhood school bus driver who later wound up on the FBI's most wanted list. (I probably didn't mention that I had a crush on him. How was I to know he was going to turn out to be a criminal?)

Such oddball facts fill all of our lives, though we may not recall them at a moment's notice. Recalling them, however, can have a lot of possibilities for the classroom. Follow the directions below and see what develops. You are likely to hear some fascinating tales, laugh a lot, and make some interesting discoveries.

Directions. Ask your students to brainstorm facts about themselves, facts that others might be surprised to know about them. The facts can be trivial, important, funny, serious—whatever. Ask them not to share their facts with one another as they brainstorm.

Of course, it may be hard to come up with unusual facts without a bit of thought. Suggest that students think about the following: places they have visited or lived, things they love, things they hate, people they have met or known, something they wish or long for, awards they have won, unusual injuries they have received, sights they have witnessed, misfortunes they have overcome, unusual facts about relatives, ancestors or friends.

After they have brainstormed for a while, give them this assignment:

> List five "facts" that you are willing to share about yourself, facts that you think are unknown to most of the class. However, there is a catch: one of the "facts" must be a lie. (Don't worry; the lies are only temporary. The class will try to guess which of your "facts" isn't really true.)

It is a good idea to give students time to think about the assignment, writing up their lists for homework and perhaps enlisting the help of family members. You might also suggest that students base their temporary lies on something that is true but about someone else.

For example, I once told a class that I met my husband because of a high school letter jacket from Afghanistan. I was attending a dance in America and saw a young man wearing a letter jacket from the high school I had attended in Afghanistan, where my father was stationed. I introduced myself and found out that we had attended the same school, but at different times. We got to talking; one thing led to another; and eventually we wound up husband and wife.

This story is not true about me, but it is true about a woman I know. Remind your students that truth often really is stranger than fiction. If they need some examples to get them thinking, you might share these facts written by one student:

- I rode my first snowmobile at the age of one month.
- My step-father once walked on the Great Wall of China.
- I was once a junior rodeo queen at the Bonneville Stampede in Idaho.
- A navy lieutenant once interviewed me as the only eyewitness to a terrible collision between two navy vehicles in Washington.

(The lie: being a junior rodeo queen.)

Here are facts from another student:

- My hard-of-hearing grandfather has ten telephones in his house, all connected to lights that go off when the phone rings.
- For six months, I had a pet tarantula named Boris.
- I was once in a Taos bookstore at the same time as Arnold Schwarzenegger and Maria Shriver.
- Once while in the attic, my dad fell through on my visiting aunt's head.

(The lie: having the pet tarantula.)

After all of the students—and you, too—have their "facts" listed, have them get into small groups to share their lists and to have others guess which of their "facts" are really lies. Many of the facts will have stories behind them, and students will want to hear the stories. When the class gets back together, ask groups to share some of the more interesting stories. Better yet, if your class is small enough, have each student share his or her "facts" with the whole class.

Finally, have your students discuss their reactions to the assignment, orally or in writing. What surprised them? What did they learn? What generalities can they make? Are there any lessons to be learned from the activity? (The questions make a perfect subject for exploration in student journals.) You might also ask each student to write the story behind one of his or her "facts." (How did it come about? Why? What were the circumstances?)

It's also fun to type up a list of facts (the true ones!) about your students and share them with other teachers and/or parents.

Using List Mania

There are several ways to use "List Mania" and "More List Mania," pages 181-182. One way is to have students get into small groups. Then pass out copies of "List Mania" to each group. Announce that students have one class period to complete as much as possible of as many lists as possible, receiving one point for each correct item on a list.

Explain that when students "grade" each other's papers, they will be able to circle any answer that is unreadable, that doesn't make sense, or that doesn't fit the list requirement. You, the teacher, will then decide whether or not to award points for those answers. Allow at least one period for list-making and a half a period for checking in class.

More "List Mania" can be used on another day. Or, if you really want to challenge students, give them "List Mania" and "More List Mania" at the same time and announce that the winner will be the first group to complete all of the lists of 15—not an easy task. (Allow at least two class periods and one night of work at home.) Or, instead of having one winner, make every group that completes all of the lists a winner.

List Mania

See if you can complete the following lists. Title each list and number the items you include, using your own paper.

1. List 15 sports.

2. List 15 annoying habits.

3. List 15 items of clothing, other than underwear.

4. List 15 green vegetables.

5. List 15 well-known animal characters from books, movies or cartoons.

6. List 15 creative excuses for not having your homework finished. (Note: "My dog ate it" is not creative!)

7. List 15 words that end in *p* and that are at least four letters long.

8. List 15 facts about your state.

9. List 15 words and phrases from baseball, other than team positions.

10. List 15 verbs that could sensibly be used instead of the word *talked*.

11. List 15 famous women, other than singers.

12. List 15 brand names of soaps.

13. List 15 musical instruments.

14. List 15 text message abbreviations and what they mean.

15. List 15 brand names of cars.

More List Mania

See if you can complete the following lists. Title each list and number the items you include, using your own paper.

1. List 15 reasons why snakes make good pets.

2. List 15 famous entertainers whose last names begin with the letter *c*.

3. List 15 animals commonly found in a zoo.

4. List 15 boys' or girls' names that begin with a vowel.

5. List 15 words that rhyme with flame.

6. List 15 kind adjectives about your teacher.

7. List 15 NFL teams.

8. List 15 countries on a continent other than yours.

9. List 15 things people commonly put on their feet.

10. List 15 autographs many people in this class would love to get.

11. List 15 characters from nursery rhymes or fairy tales.

12. List 15 colors.

13. List 15 "weather" words.

14. List 15 things you have to plug in to use.

15. List 15 summer or winter Olympic sports.

The Name Game

Many ordinary words in the English language are also common male and female names. Can you find a name to match each definition in the puzzle below? The first item is completed for you, as an example.

1. A school subject that is often a favorite _Art_____

2. Something that your parents hate to get in the mail _____

3. What people sometimes do when they are cheated in a business deal_____

4. An adjective that might be used to describe a top professional athlete _____

5. What a teacher sometimes makes with a red pen _____

6. What people often sing during the Christmas holidays _____

7. A plant used for Christmas decoration _____

8. What everyone needs, even in the worst of times _-_____

9. What a genie might do with a wish _____

10. What someone might do for an apple at Halloween _____

11. A shrub with lavender flowers _____

12. A word that often begins questions _____

13. What people often need on the back _____

14. It is good to have one of these signed before you die _____

15. What you're being when you are very open and honest _____

16. What you get when you go trick-or-treating _____

17. Used to amplify the voice _____

18. A piece of sunlight _____

19. A month noted for showers _____

20. A notch or a ship _____

21. The winner _____

22. Like a beach _____

(continued)

Ideas That Really Work! • Copyright © 2009 Cottonwood Press, Inc. • 800-864-4297 • www.cottonwoodpress.com

23. A thin, straight stick _____

24. A flower that often comes in dozens _____

25. In a marathon, you run twenty-six of them _____

26. A steel-headed spear _____

27. A white substance used as a gem _____

28. The wedding month _____

29. Something a ballet dancer needs _____

30. A spice used in cookies _____

31. What a thief does _____

32. Used for changing a tire _____

33. British slang for a policeman _____

34. A tune _____

35. Basil or parsley or oregano _____

For each item below, see if you can find a name that sounds the same as a common English word that fits the definition, but that is spelled differently. The first item is done for you.

36. What a grave digger did yesterday <u>Doug (dug)</u> _____

37. A Chevrolet or a Porsche or a Buick or a Toyota _____

38. What you might hide the house key under _____

39. Someone who never shaves _____

40. A place for working out _____

41. To grow gradually smaller _____

42. What a river does _____

43. To move or take _____

44. A strong wind _____

45. A meal in a dish _____

Answer Keys

and Sample Answers

Cars, page 20

Answers will vary. Sample answers:

	C	**A**	**R**	**S**
Makes of cars	*Chevrolet*	*Audi*	*Rolls-Royce*	*Subaru*
Adjectives that describe cars	*cool*	*awesome*	*rented*	*sleek*
Colors of cars	*cream*	*avocado*	*red*	*silver*
Verbs that tell what a car does	*careens*	*angles*	*races*	*slides*
Parts of a car	*camshaft*	*axle*	*radiator*	*speedometer*
Adverbs that tell how someone might drive a car	*cautiously*	*adeptly*	*rudely*	*safely*
Cities in America where you might drive a car	*Columbus*	*Amarillo*	*Rapid City*	*San Francisco*

The Truth vs. the Whole Truth, page 38

Answers will vary. Sample answers:

1. Mom had told him three times to empty the dishwasher. The last time, she said that if he didn't empty it, he would be grounded for a month. So he was warned.
2. The black eye was accidental. He opened the door just as she was grabbing the doorknob to come in. The door smacked her right in the face.
3. They won't let her go to school because she has been suspended for three days.
4. He picked her up at the police station because, thankfully, the police had rescued her from the man who had kidnapped her.
5. Felicia's mother only had 50 cents to lose.
6. The substitute was following the teacher's instructions. The teacher felt she needed more time to go over the material with them.
7. The daughter had already written one paper on polar bears, and the teacher felt she should expand her horizons.
8. She was with him when he was getting the tattoo, and they didn't get home until 3:00 a.m.

You Can Prove Anything If You Want, page 39

Answers will vary. Sample answers:

1. The teacher had on a new outfit on Monday. She must have come into some money.
   Her hands had some funny dye on them. She said it was from a magic marker, but maybe it was from marked money.
   She lives within a block of the robbery and would have easy access to a hiding place.
   Someone saw her in front of the bank right before it was robbed.
2. It's a *secret* training center. That's why we don't know where it is.
   I know a girl who won't say what her dad does for a living.
   I hear clicks on our phone line sometimes. I think they are training spies to listen in.
3. They always turn the lights off at the pool at night. That's so no one sees the monster.
   The custodian often carries around a bucket of something. I think he's secretly feeding the monster.
   I know someone who heard splashing at the pool one night. It was really loud, so it had to come from something huge.
   The pool manager visited Loch Ness last year. Who knows what he might have picked up?
4. No cooks would ever intentionally make food that bad. I think some spirit or ghost is getting into the food and messing it up.
   One of the cafeteria worker's hair was so wild last week. She must have seen something that made her hair stand up on end.
   We have all heard that strange squeak whenever the intercom in the cafeteria comes on. It's the moaning of a ghost.

Writing Clearly, pages 47-49

1. I do not like her.
2. I saw a cute guy and I wanted to meet him.
3. The principal announced over the intercom that students were to stop running to the lunchroom at noon.

The Party

The party in the garage was very noisy. Loud music came from the windows. Teenagers shrieked as they threw pop and chip dip at one another. When an elderly woman looked inside the garage, she gasped, shocked by what she saw. Then she screamed and fainted in the driveway.

S-S-S-S-S-Secret Message, page 50

Answers will vary. Here is one possibility:

Dear Clifford,

Can you come to a birthday party for Mr. Wiley? I know you are having fun in Italy. However, when I tell you where the party will take place, you will want to drop what you are doing and get on a train. The party will take place in beautiful Ireland.

I hope you can attend. We would love for you to be there.

Cordially,

Lady Wellington

Mythological Monsters, page 59

1. Argus: monster with a hundred eyes. Hermes put him to sleep and cut off his head. Hera scattered the eyes in a peacock's tail.
2. Cyclops: giants with one eye in the middle of the forehead.
3. Chimera: fire-breathing monster with the head of a lion, the tail of a dragon and the body of a shaggy goat.
4. Centaur: half man and half horse.
5. Cerberus: three-headed dog that guarded the entrance to the underworld.
6. Gorgons: three sisters who were so ugly they could turn anyone who looked at them into stone. They had snakes for hair, bronze hands and golden wings.
7. Griffin: had the head and wings of an eagle and the body of a lion. It guarded a great store of gold in a country called Scythia.
8. Hydra: serpent or dragon with many heads. One of the heads could not die, and the rest grew back as soon as cut off.
9. Harpies: smelly monsters, half woman and half vulture. They tear at their victims with claws.
10. Minotaur: monster with the head of a bull and the body of a man. Kept in the Labyrinth, a maze-like building, it was said to feed on human flesh.
11. Pegasus: immortal winged horse, offspring of Medusa and Poseidon.
12. Phoenix: large bird that lived exactly 500 years (or 97,200 years, according to some sources). At the end of its life cycle, the bird burned itself on a funeral pyre. A new phoenix rose from the ashes and carried the remains of its father to the sun god.
13. Sirens: sea nymphs who lived on an island. Their singing lured sailors to their shores, where the men forgot home and friends and starved to death. Or, according to some accounts, the Sirens would pounce and rip the men apart.
14. Sphinx: a creature with the body of a lion, the head of a woman, two wings and a serpent's tail.
15. Titans: strong giants who battered gods and savored human flesh.

Twenty-Five Words or Less, page 67

Answers will vary. Some possibilities:

- The deadly brown recluse spider slowly inched its way up the woman's sleeve as she innocently snoozed in her overstuffed chair.
- As the Monarch butterfly balanced on the exotic pink blossom, its delicate orange and velvet black wings fluttered in the gentle May breeze.
- The mossy slime oozed out from under the lid of the 2002 cottage cheese container lurking in the back of the refrigerator.

One Syllable Challenge, page 68

Answers will vary. One possibility:

I love cats much more than dogs. They warm my heart when they sit on my lap and purr. They are smart. They know how to get what they want with a stare or the bat of a paw. They do as they please, and that makes me mad once in a while. Still, it shows they have a mind of their own and can't be bought off with a treat. A dog, though, will sell its soul for a pat on the head.

Toenails and Juice Boxes, 69

Answers will vary. One possibility:

Kitty scratching in her litter,
First one way and then the other.
Sure would like to hide it better.
Think I'll put it under cover.

Kitty's paws are pooper scoopers,
Flinging clumps both left and right,
Noisy as a whirly chopper.
Think I'll put her out tonight.

Ridiculous Similes, page 70

Answers will vary. One possibility:

1. The garbage disposal churned on like a thundercloud rumbling.
2. The white iPod wires coming out of his ears looked like long strands of overcooked spaghetti.
3. After the wax job, the car looked as smooth and glossy as a just-opened container of vanilla yogurt.
4. The mountain climber hung on the side of the cliff like a piece of lint on a sweater.
5. The child was as tense as a toaster about to pop.
6. From high atop the mountain, the lake looked like a black button sewn onto a crisp green shirt.
7. As I closed my eyes to take a nap, the calming silence enveloped me like a bun covering a hamburger.
8. The toothbrush bristles were as worn-down as the treads on an old pair of sneakers.
9. She tried to pay attention to the teacher, but her boredom smothered her like thick, sticky peanut butter.
10. The mop swept into the room's nooks and crannies like a lobster looking for a place to hide.

The Candidate, page 74

Answers will vary. Here's one example:

Presidential candidate Sandra Nation strolled confidently onto the stage as the audience members stomped their feet, applauded, and chanted "Sandra Nation! Sandra Nation!" She gripped the sides of the podium, leaned into the messy tangle of microphones, and said, "The world is finally ready for a female president!" The crowd exploded with cheers and tossed red, white, and blue confetti into the air. Nation's crazy-curly hair caught a bunch of it, but she just flicked it away. "Welcome to the future!" she said, looking out at the sea of supporters. Thousands of balloons cascaded from the ceiling as the crowd surged forward, shouting, "Nation for our nation! Nation for our nation!"

Moving My Curfew-Questions, page 82

1. For several reasons, it is clearly time to move my curfew to 12:30 on weekends.
2. (a) I need practice handling the greater freedom that goes along with being an adult.
   (b) I am an active student.
   (c) I can be trusted to handle a later curfew.

3. When they go away to college, some students can't handle the extra freedom. They get into trouble partying too much, neglecting school work and sometimes even breaking the law.

4. (a) Other students must take over for me when I have to leave early, and this is unfair to them.
   (b) I am embarrassed because my friends think my parents don't trust me.

5. (a) I have never been in serious trouble, either at school or in the community.
   (b) I hold a part-time job and still manage to maintain a "B" average in school.
   (c) When it's my turn to cook dinner at home, I always remember to do it and have it on the table on time.

6. It is clear that my curfew should be moved to 12:30. (OR) I hope you will act right away to change my curfew.

I'll Take a Cat—Questions, page 84

1. Cats make better pets than dogs.

2. (a) Cats don't make as much mess.
   (b) Cats are more suitable for urban life.
   (c) A cat's love is easier to take.

3. For (a): Dogs chew anything they can get a hold of; cats chew only their dinners; dogs are a mess to housebreak; cats just need to be shown the litter box; dogs gallop through the house with muddy feet; cats lick themselves clean.
   For (b): Dogs have to be walked; cats walk themselves; dogs bother the neighbors by barking, munching tomatoes from their gardens, leaving piles and spreading garbage all over; cats stroll politely, bothering no one.
   For (c): Puppies jump on you and ruin your tights; a cat rubs softly against your legs; dogs give wet, slobbery kisses; a cat climbs in your lap, cuddles and purrs.

4. But when compared to cats, they come up losers in the pet department.

Introduction to Plenzenarks, page 89

Answers will vary. Some possibilities:

The attention-getter:

Did you know that the future of the planet depends on something called "plenzenarks"? Most people don't know about plenzenarks and have no idea how important they are, but if they did, they would make them their top priority. The most effective way to save our planet is to make people aware that plenzenarks exist.

A quotation:

"Anyone who doubts the existence of plenzenarks is living in a dream world," says Newton Figgleswart, professor of nuclear physics. "They are very real, and they are very dangerous." Professor Figgleswart has made it his mission to spread the word about plenzenarks.

An anecdote:

Plenzenarks saved my little brother's life. He was born with a rare disease that has no known cure—until now. He participated in a clinical trial that uses plenzenarks to treat various rare diseases.

Plenzenarks neutralized his disease in a mere month and he is now completely normal. I believe that the discovery of plenzenarks will prove to be the most important scientific advancement of the last century.

A list or series:

Plenzenarks make up ninety-nine percent of the Earth's atmosphere. They make up ninety-five percent of the world's soil. They are in eighty-five percent of the Earth's water. But only one percent of the world's population knows what plenzenarks are. Unless we can raise more awareness about these vital particles, our planet is in serious danger.

Present the problem:

The biggest issue we face today is the disappearance of plenzenarks. Every person on Earth is affected by this problem. Unfortunately, most people still question the existence of plenzenarks. If we are to solve this crisis, we must convince people that plenzenarks exist.

Who-what-when-where-why-how:

Last week, scientists at the Center for New Discoveries in Washington, D.C. found evidence of new particles called plenzenarks. The scientists were experimenting with DNA when they accidentally stumbled upon the plenzenarks. This discovery is sure to change the world as we know it.

What Is Plagiarism?, page 98

1. **P.** (*There are only very minor changes from the original.*)
2. OK
3. **P.** (*The first sentence is almost identical to the original, and the second sentence is identical to one in the original paragraph.*)
4. OK
5. OK
6. **P.** (*Whole sentences are copied, with original sentences added in between.*)
7. **P.** (*Although quotation marks are used, there is no credit given to the source.*)

Parts of Speechless, page 99

Answers will vary. Some possibilities:

1. (no pronouns) A little boy and a little girl were playing fetch with their golden retriever puppy. The little boy would throw a stick and the puppy would fetch the stick. Then the little girl would try throwing the stick, but the puppy would just jump up and lick the little girl's face. The puppy could smell ice cream on the little girl's face and preferred to shower the little girl with puppy kisses, hoping to get a taste of the ice cream. The puppy thought that was much better than chasing some stupid stick.

2. (no adjectives) Cheri went looking for Sophie the cat but couldn't find her anywhere. She called and called but Sophie did not appear. Cheri looked in all the closets and drawers and under all the beds and chairs. Finally she heard a meow that sounded far away. She followed the sound and it led her to a window where Sophie had pushed the screen loose and had crawled onto the roof and could not get back in. Cheri recognized the terror in the eyes of Sophie. She quickly scooped Sophie back into the house and was immediately rewarded with lots of purring.

3. (no prepositions) There is a great place to eat family meals. It is our kitchen. The food is always good and cooked to the right temperature. Meals are the time we share our daily stories and experiences. We laugh. We think seriously. We get scolded. We respect each other. It is a time we all feel connected and loved. Did I say the food is good?

4. (no conjunctions) We have our own battle in our house. Each family member wants to be named "The Best Wii Snowboarder," an award we invented. We compete an hour daily after dinner. It was tricky at first, learning to hold the Wii controller the right way. This is how each move is counted. We had to learn to move our feet correctly. Each slide is a point. Each knee bent the right way is a point. Each body sway is a point. It is really fun. We laugh. We get frustrated. We exercise.

Alphabet Adjectives, page 101

Answers will vary. Here is one possibility:

When <u>a</u>gile George got married, <u>b</u>eautiful, talented Mary became his bride. The couple's unusual parents, however, made the wedding a <u>c</u>urious event.

Mary's father showed up in a <u>d</u>umb-looking suit instead of his usually <u>e</u>legant attire. His wife showed up in a <u>f</u>rumpy green dress in a <u>h</u>orrible cocker spaniel puppy print, with an <u>i</u>mmense full skirt, a <u>j</u>agged hemline, and <u>k</u>icky pleats. Her <u>l</u>emon-colored hat had <u>m</u>aroon flowers perched on top, and her <u>n</u>ovelty earrings were made out of <u>o</u>ld golf balls.

With a <u>p</u>atient smile, the <u>q</u>uiet couple nodded at Mary's parents and then turned to greet George's mother and father. His father wore a <u>r</u>ed <u>s</u>potted sweater and <u>t</u>weed pants that were <u>u</u>gly and too short. His mother wore a <u>v</u>iolet evening gown with <u>w</u>orn-out loafers. She carried <u>X</u>eroxed photographs of her darling boy as a baby. As she passed out the pictures of <u>y</u>oung George, she began, with <u>z</u>estful energy, to sing, "Baby face. You've got the cutest little baby face..."

Verbs Rule! Groking It, page 103

Testing whether or not they "grok" it:

1. Temperatures rise.	12. Computers crash.
4. Parents yell.	13. Photocopiers jam.
5. Girls giggle.	14. Storms rage.
7. Snow falls.	17. Parents listen.
9. Noses twitch.	18. Brothers fight.
10. Eyes close.	19. Credits roll.

Hyperbole, page 108

Answers will vary. Some possibilities:

1. It's so hot that even the asphalt is complaining.
2. It's so cold that you can feel your thoughts freeze.
3. Amber's jokes are so funny that it takes you a week to stop laughing.
4. The movie was so boring that even the popcorn fell asleep.
5. Chuck is so handsome that even his mirror has a crush on him.
6. Lisa was thirsty enough to drink all the soda from every 7-11 on the planet.
7. My mom was so embarrassed she could have crawled inside her purse.
8. The instructions were so confusing that even Einstein would have given up.
9. Antonio was so happy that if you told him the sun was going to explode, he would smile.
10. Mrs. Hampton was so rich that she could afford to put every ant in the world on her payroll.
11. The jack-o'-lantern was so big that it would have tipped our house over if we had put it on the porch.
12. The boy was so small that even a flea couldn't see him.
13. The man was so angry that he could have crumpled a car in his fist.
14. Roxy is so trendy even the air she breathes has to have a designer name.
15. Barb is so shy that she blushes when she writes her own name.
16. The band was so loud that aliens from another planet called to complain.
17. My brother's room is so messy that animals thought to be extinct have been discovered in there.
18. The cake was so sweet, my teeth rotted on the spot.
19. Sean's sister is so hyper, hummingbirds find her annoying.
20. Libby is so smart that she makes a group of rocket scientists look like a class of remedial preschoolers.

Prepositions Are Boring Words, pages 125-126

More practice with prepositions:

1. (at a desk) (at the back) (of a math classroom)
2. (at the girl) (in the next row) (beside a window) (in her notebook)
3. (with a barrette) (in it)
4. (at Joshua)
5. none
6. (on page 21)
7. (at his book)
8. (of her notebook) (to Joshua)
9. (at home) (by itself) (on the floor) (of his closet)
10. (At the local Pizza Hut) (beside a girl) (with a rose tattoo) (with pepperoni and mushrooms)

Activities with Adjectives, page 128

B.

1. *A* and *green* describe dragon. *The* and *dark* describe castle. *The, beautiful* and *sleeping* describe princess.

2. *A*, *giant* and *fuzzy* describe spider. *Chad's* describes hair.
3. *The*, *tall* and *handsome* describe boy. *A*, *brown* and *leather* describe jacket. *The* and *math* describe classroom.

C.
Adjectives (in order of appearance): *his, the, the, movie, a, giant-sized, buttered, two, small, the, overhead, their, the, wide, a, familiar, his, little, her, best, the.*

Using Quotation Marks, pages 131-132

1. I.
2. D. Jim's mother said, "I will ground you for a month if you don't clean up this pigpen of a room. Today!"
3. D. "My sister always wants anchovies on her pizza," said Kristen. "The rest of us gag at the smell of them."
4. D. "I hate boys who are conceited," remarked Melanie. "I also hate it when they show off all the time."
5. I.
6. I.
7. D. Michael didn't have much confidence. "I'm going to flunk. I'm going to flunk. I'm going to flunk," he repeated over and over to himself as he took the math test.

The Apostrophe, page 134-136

What are contractions?
Answers will vary. Some possibilities: *wasn't, weren't, isn't, doesn't.*

Practice writing possessives
1. Tammy's new dress
2. Mary's anger toward Bill
3. the nation's capital
4. the child's puppy

Plural nouns
1. the family's Christmas party
2. the two babies' large crib
3. the three families' Christmas party
4. the two students' locker
5. the women's department

Sentence Structure, page 139

Part A
Main sentences:
1. ~~The students at Washington Junior High scored well on the district physical education test.~~
2. Tammy drove her friends to the dance.

3. The speaker began his talk with a joke.
4. The first grader eagerly walked to school with his mother.
5. The storm raged across the city.
6. A dead frog lay on the table in biology class.
7. Jason worked hard to improve his grade in science.
8. Dozens of boxes crashed to the floor.
9. My best friend Linda decided that she was dying of thirst.
10. The new student walked into the classroom.

Part B

Main sentences:
1. Cruz dropped his books all over the floor.
2. Angela's favorite teacher was just elected teacher of the year.
3. Steve sat quietly at his desk.
4. Her mother sat at the table.
5. Most teachers don't particularly like to grade papers.
6. Most students secretly enjoy homework.
7. Jo Ann went to the game. There she bought a huge tub of popcorn.

Practice with Semicolons, page 144

1. Elizabeth loved Scott; Scott loved Karen.
2. Correct.
3. Emily knew she should be studying for her history test; however, she really wanted to pull the covers over her head and go to sleep.
4. I never saw a purple cow; I never hope to see one.
5. Marie likes to do the dishes right after dinner; her husband Michael likes to put them off until morning.
6. Correct.
7. Teachers are wise; students are not.
8. Correct.

Thank Heaven for Pronouns, page 145

Jack was walking with his cafeteria tray when he saw Raina sitting at a table with an empty chair beside her. He smiled at her, and she smiled back. He asked if he could sit down with her. She smiled shyly and said, "Sure."

They ate quietly for a moment, and then Jack said, "Would you like some of my Tater Tots?"

Raina said, "Yes." Then she said, "My friends are having a pizza party for my birthday on Friday. Do you want to join us?"

He said, "Sure. I think going to your party sounds great."

Patrick was sitting beside Jack and Raina. He couldn't stand it anymore. "Please use pronouns!" he yelled. "Stop sounding like idiots!"

September Brain Strain, page 150

Answers will vary. Sample answer:

2. Samantha Evans pretended to eat many beans.

   Eric Rodriguez read Erin's book.

   Many elephants try pouting every Saturday.

   Subtotal: 50
3. Emily Edwards estimates errors easily on elevators.

   Subtotal: 50
4. Some pigs try munching broccoli.

   Rhonda Reid brought many tropical pink snakes.

   Subtotal: 60
5. Some estimates predict tornadoes each month, beginning early.

   Rodney races each bicyclist.

   Monday, Edward tries parachuting.

   Emilio sings.

   Subtotal: 40

Total Score: 200

Not for the Squeamish, page 153

Answers will vary. Sample answer:

On Tuesday morning, after a <u>squall</u> damaged area businesses, the police <u>squad</u> was called to <u>squelch</u> a <u>squabble</u> at the <u>Squirting Squid</u> Restaurant in Harbor <u>Square</u>. According to eyewitnesses, the restaurant owner was outside cleaning his restaurant sign with a <u>squeegee</u> when a group of protesters showed up. Apparently, the protesters were <u>squeamish</u> about the name of the restaurant. "We don't condone cruelty to sea creatures," one protester said. "This restaurant seems to believe it's okay to <u>squeeze</u> and <u>squish</u> a <u>squirming</u>, <u>squiggling</u> squid until it squirts ink! We demand that the restaurant change its name and stop <u>squandering</u> our natural resources."

Eyewitnesses say a fight ensued when protesters entered the restaurant and began throwing fake rubber squids at patrons who were dining on "<u>Squash</u> Surprise," the special of the day. When the restaurant owner heard <u>squeals</u> from inside his restaurant, he <u>squinted</u> through the window and saw his patrons being pelted by the protesters. He immediately ran in and called police. "I <u>squirreled</u> away money for 30 years to turn this <u>squalid</u> building into a <u>squeaky</u> clean restaurant, and I'm not about to be run off by a few protesters!" said the angry restaurant owner.

Sports Mania, page 160

Answers will vary. Sample answers on next page:

20 different sports:

1. football
2. basketball
3. tennis
4. volleyball
5. wrestling
6. skiing
7. iceskating
8. golf
9. swimming
10. bobsledding
11. bowling
12. karate
13. boxing
14. archery
15. fencing
16. gymnastics
17. hockey
18. soccer
19. speed skating
20. kayaking

20 well-known athletes:

1. Cal Ripkin, Jr.
2. Peyton Manning
3. Pete Sampras
4. Tiger Woods
5. George Foreman
6. Michael Jordan
7. Matt Holiday
8. Michael Phelps
9. Andre Agassi
10. Lance Armstrong
11. Sasha Cohen
12. Bonnie Blair
13. Sanya Richards
14. Tracy Caulkins
15. Shawn Johnson
16. Maria Sharapova
17. Gabrielle Reece
18. Annika Sorenstam
19. Hannah Teter
20. Julia Mancuso

20 common terms:

1. home run: baseball
2. field goal: football
3. rink: hockey
4. kickoff: football
5. foul: football, baseball
6. center ice: hockey
7. basket: basketball
8. yellow card: soccer
9. penalty box: hockey
10. free-throw: basketball
11. blocking: football
12. traveling: basketball
13. blitz: football
14. drop ball: soccer
15. fumble: football
16. pitcher: baseball
17. dunk: basketball
18. puck: hockey
19. save: hockey
20. bullpen: baseball

20 team names:

1. Oakland Raiders
2. New York Yankees
3. Detroit Pistons
4. Los Angeles Kings
5. Duke Blue Devils
6. Colorado Rockies
7. Indiana Hoosiers
8. Pittsburgh Steelers
9. Phoenix Suns
10. New York Rangers
11. Tampa Bay Buccaneers
12. Michigan Wolverines
13. Green Bay Packers
14. Boston Bruins
15. Colorado Avalanche
16. Tennessee Volunteers
17. St. Louis Cardinals
18. Detroit Tigers
19. Chicago Cubs
20. Texas Longhorns

20 places:

1. Madison Square Garden
2. Conseco Fieldhouse
3. Minute Maid Park
4. Yankee Stadium
5. LA Coliseum
6. Invesco Field
7. Wrigley Field
8. Belmont Park
9. Churchill Downs
10. AT &T Park
11. Fenway Park
12. Wimbledon
13. Citi Field
14. Lambeau Field
15. Dodger Stadium
16. Rose Bowl
17. Wachovia Spectrum
18. Pepsi Center
19. Daytona Speedway
20. Indianapolis Speedway

20 things a person might do in a physical education class:

1. jumping jacks
2. somersaults
3. push-ups
4. sit-ups
5. squat thrusts
6. chin-ups
7. toe touches
8. log rolls
9. pull-ups
10. play kick ball
11. play dodge ball
12. run laps
13. pick teams
14. jump rope
15. sweat
16. skip
17. play field hockey
18. swim laps
20. climb the rope

20 things used in sports for "make up a sports category of your own":

1. racket
2. ball
3. tee
4. puck
5. helmet
6. mat
7. paddle
8. kayak
9. life jacket
10. sail
11. net
12. golf clubs
13. bicycle
14. track
15. court
16. gloves
17. race car
18. saddle
19. swimsuit
20. tennis shoes

Spring 100 Challenge, page 167

Answers will vary. Here are a few sample 10 point sentences:

1. Small puppies ran into Nancy's garden.
2. Several people rode in new gondolas.
3. Sam paraded right into Nate's garage.
4. Sue poured red ink near George.
5. Sally's parents readily invited ninety guests.
6. Spring pruning really increases new growth.
7. Stupid press releases impede news gathering.

Longer and Longer, page 172

Answers will vary. Sample answer:

1. I am the only third grader.
2. My mom said, "Haley, forget Anthony!"
3. The girl tells Oliver unusual accounts.
4. Then Betty glided through sunlight.
5. Young pandas spotted friendly, talkative zookeepers.

(Total: 156 points)

Vocabulary Puzzle, page 173

1. Yagi doesn't belong because it is a short wave antenna and the others are types of plants.
2. tack, taco, tact, tail, tape, tart, taxi, team, tern, test, tick, tide, tier, tiki, time, tire, toad, toga, toll, tomb, tome, tune, turf, tusk, tutu
3. cow, gentle, immaculate, improbable, incredible, indented, industrious, inevitable, ink, insight, intestine
4. An ocelot wouldn't belong because it is an animal, not an instrument.
5. Paraquat might be considered unsafe because it is a toxic herbicide.
6. When the grumpy old man met the kind old lady, his heart skipped a beat and he fell in love.
7. Articulate would best describe a good speaker because it means expressing yourself clearly or effectively.
8. Aquarius, Aries, Cancer, Capricorn, Gemini, Leo, Libra, Pisces, Sagittarius, Scorpio, Taurus, Virgo
9. An adze is a type of axe for shaping wood, and it might be used by a carpenter, a wood sculptor, or a boatbuilder.
10. The carpenter used a rabbet joint to fit the boards together on the rabbit cage.
11. One syllable: squelch, knoll; Two syllables: mollusk, flapjack, grommet, emu, goblin, oblong, haddock, smidgen, flipper; Three syllables: emulate, pendulum, spatula, peppercorn; Four syllables: salamander
12. A spelunker explores and studies caves. A numismatist collects and studies coins. I'd rather be a numismatist because searching for valuable coins would be fun. I wouldn't want to be a spelunker because caves are scary.
13. Sweltering doesn't belong in the list because it describes heat and the other terms describe cold.
14. daffodil, pencil, taxi, banana, canary, cheese, corn, squash, lemon, pineapple
15. You should never use "excape" or "expecially" because they are incorrect. The correct spellings are escape and especially.

Whining, page 174

1. I hate it when the pizza crust is soggy. I also hate it when the hot cheese burns the roof of your mouth.
2. I hate it when you think you're opening a plastic container of leftover tuna and it turns out to be a container of something green with purple fuzzy mold growing on it.
3. I hate it when the seatbelt in the car hits me in the neck because I'm too short.
4. I hate it when I can't find the remote control.
5. I hate it when my sister is watching something stupid and won't give me the remote control.
6. I hate it when my mom puts tofu in things and hopes I won't notice.
7. I hate it when the pepperoni on the pizza isn't evenly divided and I get a slice with only one piece of pepperoni on it.
8. I hate it when it's time to go and my mom can't find her keys.
9. I hate it when my cat upchucks a hairball on my bed.
10. I hate it when someone finishes the milk and puts the empty carton back in the refrigerator.
11. I hate it when my parents try to act cool around my friends.
12. I hate it when I get a pimple right between my eyebrows.
13. I hate it when I get a pimple anywhere.
14. I hate it when someone steps on the back of my shoe and makes it come off.
15. I hate it when my parents are on a diet and we have to eat baked fish.
16. I hate it when my parents turn off my stereo and say, "Aaaaah . . . . silence!"
17. I hate how my friend eats her Reese's Peanut Butter Cups by nibbling the chocolate completely off before she gets to the peanut butter part.
18. I hate it when my dad asks questions like, "Who is this Tommy Hilfiger?"
19. I hate it when my sister gets on the phone and it kicks me off the Internet.
20. I hate how my sister chews off all of her fingernails instead of cutting them like a normal person.
21. I hate it when the mashed potatoes touch the peas on my plate.
22. I hate it when my shoelaces get caught in my bicycle spokes.
23. I hate it when my mom makes me bring my little brother along when my friends and I go to the mall.
24. I hate when I'm trying to read and the neighbor's dog won't stop barking.
25. I hate it when my teacher makes me write a list of all the things I hate.

Lipograms, page 176

Answers will vary. Sample answers:

1. After snoozing on the soft rug and eating some herbs that appeal to felines, my goofy kitty likes to run after a mouse or two.
2. Billy regularly enjoys romping with his energetic puppy and throwing a plastic disc that he can catch and retrieve.
3. Julie would rather not do homework on the weekend in the evening, due to her fatigue after being at college all week.
4. Sam thought he might take a stroll around the lake, but the blustery conditions prevented it.

English, page 177

Answers will vary. Sample answers:

	E	N	G	L	I	S	H
Boys' names	Eric	Ned	Greg	Larry	Ivan	Sam	Henry
Five-letter words	enter	night	groan	locks	imply	sword	happy
Animals	elephant	newt	gorilla	lion	iguana	sloth	hare
Sports	equestrian racing	Nordic skiing	golf	lacrosse	ice hockey	soccer	hang gliding
Proper nouns	Empire State Building	Norway	Georgia	Louisiana	Israel	Spanish	Hollywood
Things with wheels	engine	Nissan	go-cart	locomotive	Isuzu	stock car	Honda
Fruits	elderberry	nectarine	grape	lime	Italian tomato	strawberry	huckleberry
Girls' names	Emily	Nora	Gwen	Lisa	Irene	Sally	Heather
Words that end in *e*	eliminate	none	gripe	leave	idle	stone	haste
Countries of the world	England	Norway	Greenland	Lithuania	Ireland	Spain	Holland
Words that might be used as verbs (action words)	enter	nod	grab	leap	illuminate	slither	hop
Cartoon characters	Eugene	Jimmy Neutron	Goofy	Lisa	Itchy	SpongeBob SquarePants	Homer
Movie titles	Ella Enchanted	Naked Gun	Groundhog Day	Lord of the Rings	Indiana Jones	Shrek	Harry Potter
Last names of nationally-known athletes	Els, Ernie	Nowitzki, Dirk	Griffey, Ken	Leslie, Lisa	Iverson, Allen	Sakic, Joe	Hamm, Mia

List Mania, page, page 181

Answers will vary. Sample answers:

1. soccer, baseball, football, tennis, swimming, rugby, skiing, golf, bowling, boxing, wrestling, hockey, basketball, cycling, volleyball.
2. grinding teeth, chewing with mouth open, cracking knuckles, saying "like" all the time, burping, tapping fingers, chewing gum loudly, sniffing, whistling, chewing fingernails, picking nose, humming same song, saying "huh?" all the time, smoking, chewing tobacco.
3. shirt, pants, blouse, suit, shorts, socks, skirt, dress, jacket, sweatshirt, coat, T-shirt, pajamas, belt, hat.

4. broccoli, asparagus, green beans, lettuce, chives, brussels sprouts, cabbage, zucchini, bean sprouts, artichoke, peas, spinach, celery, cucumber, lima beans.

5. Dumbo, Mickey Mouse, Donald Duck, Mighty Mouse, Big Bird, Miss Piggy, Bullwinkle, Snoopy, Garfield, Goofy, Bambi, Thumper, Kermit, Old Yeller, Hobbes.

6. (Kids should have no trouble with this one!)

7. drip, strip, flip, snap, strap, clap, flap, trap, wrap, chip, chap, drop, slop, creep, sleep.

8. Answers will vary, according to the state lived in.

9. balk, batting clean-up, "Texas" leaguer, full count, foul ball, squeeze play, bunt, force out, on deck, RBI, home run, bull pen, dugout, curve ball, double play.

10. chattered, gabbed, gossiped, shared, argued, babbled, lectured, droned, explained, said, mumbled, shouted, spoke, conversed, discussed.

11. Diane Sawyer, Mother Theresa, Pat Schroeder, Susan B. Anthony, Elizabeth Taylor, Madame Curie, Anita Hill, Queen Elizabeth, Sally Field, Oprah Winfrey, Bonnie Blair, Emily Dickinson, Hillary Rodham Clinton, Whoopi Goldberg, Barbara Bush.

12. Dial, Irish Spring, Zest, Joy, Dawn, Tide, All, Ivory, Caress, Noxema, Neutrogena, Dove, Cheer, Coast, Palmolive.

13. clarinet, accordion, guitar, piano, organ, flute, violin, trumpet, trombone, bass, recorder, banjo, mandolin, drum, tuba.

14. BF (best friend), BFN (Bye for now), 10X (Thanks), JK (Just kidding), C&G (chuckle & grin), CU (See you), CUL (See you later), D8 (date), DIKU (Do I know you?), LOL (laughing out loud, or lots of luck), P911 (parent alert, change subject) LY (Love you), SWAK (sealed with a kiss), UOM (You owe me), WOA (work of art).

15. Buick, Chrysler, Dodge, Honda, Hummer, Jeep, Kia, Mercury, Nissan, Prius, Saab, Smart, Subaru, Toyota, Volkswagen.

More List Mania, page 182

Answers will vary.

1. No need to walk. Don't need much food. Don't need litter box. Don't bark. Don't need a fenced yard. If they die, can make them into boots. Can curl up beside you. Can help control mice. Travel well inside luggage. Shed only once a year. Will eat cheap food. No one else in neighborhood has one. Can use snake holes for golf. Handy for Adam and Eve skits. Handy for rain dances.

2. Tom Cruise, Kevin Costner, Bill Cosby, Johnny Carson, Joe Cocker, Nicholas Cage, Natalie Cole, Mariah Carey, Tracy Chapman, Michael Caine, Ray Charles, Dana Carvey, Glenn Close, John Candy, Macaulay Culkin.

3. elephant, lion, tiger, giraffe, bear, panther, zebra, rhinoceros, gorilla, hippopotamus, cheetah, chimpanzee, hyena, kangaroo, leopard.

4. Ed, Ophelia, Abby, Andrew, Igor, Ursula, Emma, Adam, Allan, Ellen, Oscar, Evan, Eleanor, Avery, Orville.

5. game, same, tame, lame, name, dame, fame, blame, claim, came, maim, shame, aim, frame, exclaim.

6. beautiful, helpful, understanding, caring, brilliant, inspirational, lovely, talented, clever, patient, funny, witty, perceptive, creative, interesting.

7. Dolphins, Oilers, Steelers, Broncos, Chiefs, Seahawks, Cowboys, Giants, Redskins, Bears, Lions, Vikings, Rams, Eagles, Packers.

8. Afghanistan, Belgium, Denmark, Egypt, France, Greece, Iraq, Ireland, Japan, Kenya, Nigeria, Pakistan, Rwanda, Peru, Zambia.

9. socks, sandals, nail polish, pumps, loafers, huaraches, sneakers, high heels, nylons, wingtips, slippers, boots, clogs, thongs, moccasins.

10. (Students will have no trouble with this one.)

11. Miss Muffet, Rapunzel, Rumplestiltskin, Old King Cole, Old Mother Hubbard, Snow White, Jack, Jill, Little Red Riding Hood, Little Bo-peep, Georgie Porgie, Jack Sprat, Humpty Dumpty, Wee Willie Winkie, Little Jack Horner.

12. red, yellow, blue, black, orange, green, purple, violet, brown, turquoise, pink, magenta, olive, chartreuse, tan.

13. tornado, snow, rain, sleet, typhoon, hail, hurricane, blizzard, front, temperature, heat wave, slush, cyclone, monsoon, sunny.

14. washer, dryer, dishwasher, toaster, hairdryer, electric razor, mixer, blender, curling iron, computer, answering machine, lamp, iron, television, stereo.

15. diving, swimming, archery, badminton, basketball, boxing, canoeing, fencing, field hockey, curling, gymnastics, judo, rowing, sailing, volleyball.

The Name Game, pages 183-184

1. Art	10. Bob	19. April	28. June	37. Otto (auto)
2. Bill	11. Heather	20. Nick	29. Grace	38. Matt (mat)
3. Sue	12. May	21. Victor	30. Ginger	39. Harry (hairy)
4. Rich	13. Pat	22. Sandy	31. Rob	40. Jim (gym)
5. Mark	14. Will	23. Rod	32. Jack	41. Wayne (wane)
6. Carol	15. Frank	24. Rose	33. Bobby	42. Flo (flow)
7. Holly	16. Candy	25. Miles	34. Melody	43. Carrie (carry)
8. Hope	17. Mike	26. Lance	35. Herb	44. Gail (gale)
9. Grant	18. Ray	27. Pearl	36. Doug (dug)	45. Stu (stew)

About the Author. Cheryl Miller Thurston is a former teacher and the author of many books, plays, songs, and musicals. She lives in Loveland, Colorado, with her husband and two pampered cats.